ATARI® SOUND AND GRAPHICS

HERB MOORE
JUDY LOWER
BOB ALBRECHT

Dymax Corporation
Menlo Park, California

1807 1982 175 YEARS OF PUBLISHING

John Wiley & Sons, Inc.

New York • Chichester • Brisbane • Toronto • Singapore

Publisher: Judy V. Wilson
Editor: Dianne Littwin
Composition and Make-up: Cobb/Dunlop, Inc.

Cover graphic: "Hexrotate" by Michael Dubno and Computer Center New York, photographed on the ATARI 800 Computer at Digibyte, New York City.

Library of Congress Cataloging in Publication Data

Moore, Herb, 1944–
Atari sound and graphics.

(A Wiley self-teaching guide)
Includes index.
1. Atari 400 (Computer)—Programming. 2. Atari 800 (Computer)—Programming. 3. Computer sound processing. 4. Computer graphics. I. Lower, Judy. II. Albrecht, Bob, 1930– III. Title. IV. Series.
QA76.8.A8M66 001.64'1 81-23111
ISBN 0-471-09593-1 AACR2

Printed in the United States of America

82 83 10 9 8 7 6 5 4 3 2 1

Contents

To the Reader

Assuming no prior knowledge of computers, this book serves as your "road map" into the world of ATARI* Computer sound and color graphics. While exploring, you will learn to speak the most commonly used computer language in existence today: BASIC. It is a simple language to learn and most computers (large or small) can be programmed using BASIC.

ATARI Sound and Graphics emphasizes recreation and artistic expression. As you use this book you will not only learn a number of "useful" things about computers, but will also experience the pleasures of creating beautiful colors, shapes, and sounds with your ATARI Computer.

With this book you can easily learn to create exciting sound effects, some of which you may have already heard in various arcade games. And since the graphics capabilities of the ATARI 400 and ATARI 800 Computers are not only powerful but easily accessible, you will also find yourself creating colorful figures very quickly.

Later in the book you will get a taste of music theory and will create your own melodies and be able to see them play on the screen.

ATARI Sound and Graphics is meant to be used, along with the ATARI 400 or ATARI 800 Computer so you can try each new concept as it is presented. After all, seeing and hearing each new sound or color produced by the computer is the part that's most fun. The fundamental grammar and logic of ATARI® BASIC is presented in a step-by-step fashion, with an emphasis on interaction and exploration with your computer. As you learn new concepts and techniques you will often be encouraged to apply them to your own artistic creations.

So whether you are a teacher wishing to prepare audio-visual aids for your classroom, an artist or musician seeking to explore the world of computer sound and graphics, or someone who just wants to play with the computer, this book and an ATARI 400 or ATARI 800 Computer will provide you with hours of pleasure and a great amount of useful knowledge.

Now take a look at "How to Use This Book," and then go on to learn about ATARI Computer sound and graphics!

How to Use This Book

With this book's self-instructional format, you'll be actively involved in learning BASIC for the ATARI Computer. The material in each chapter is presented in short sections, each of which teaches you something new about ATARI® BASIC and gives you a question or asks you to write a program. Correct answers are given following the dashed line. For the most effective learning we urge you to use a thick paper to keep the answers out of sight until you have written your answer.

You will learn best if you actually write out the answers and try the programs out on the computer. The questions are carefully designed to call your attention to important points in the examples and explanations, and to help you learn to apply what is being explained or demonstrated.

The Self-Test at the end of each chapter can be used as a review of the material covered in the chapter. You may test yourself immediately after reading the chapter. Or you may wish to read a chapter, take a break, and save the Self-Test as a review before you begin the next chapter. To go further in applying what you have learned, do the Challenges following the Self-Test. Answers are not given for the Challenges.

This is a self-contained book for learning ATARI Computer sound and graphics, but what you learn will be theoretical until you actually sit down at a computer terminal and apply your knowledge of the computer language and programming techniques. So we strongly recommend that you and this book get together with an ATARI computer.

Introduction

The language you will be learning in this book is ATARI® BASIC, a very simple form of an English-based language for computers. BASIC is understood by many computers. ATARI BASIC also has some special vocabulary for creating sound and color graphics.

As you use this book, keep in mind a few things about your interaction with your ATARI 400 or 800 Computer.

First, remember you are learning ways to tell your computer what you want it to do. You'll learn to speak a language the computer understands. Computer programmers of all skill levels think in terms of computer languages.

Second, although this book focuses mainly on sound and graphics, you will also learn many skills that will be valuable to you as you find other ways to use your ATARI 400 or 800 Computer.

You will learn many introductory programming techniques. Many of the sounds you will learn to create can be found in today's arcade games, and the graphics can be equally innovative—creations that are fun and exciting as you devise your own ways to use them. If you wish to learn more conventional music, we suggest you also consider the Music Composer® and the Video Easel ®, programs for the ATARI Computer.

When you are learning to speak another language—such as Spanish or French—the more you practice and learn, the more you understand. The same is true with ATARI BASIC. As you begin to understand the machine more fully, you will find it easier to get the machine to do what you want it to do.

Remember also, if the machine doesn't understand you, it's not because of any lack of intelligence on your part. The computer has a very specific language, and if you start to speak another dialect or become too subtle, it can easily become confused.

Be patient with your computer. And most of all, remember it's not the computer telling you what to do, but you telling the computer what to do!

CHAPTER ONE

Getting Started— The Sound Statement

When you turn on the ATARI* Computer,** you'll know that it is ready when the screen looks like this:

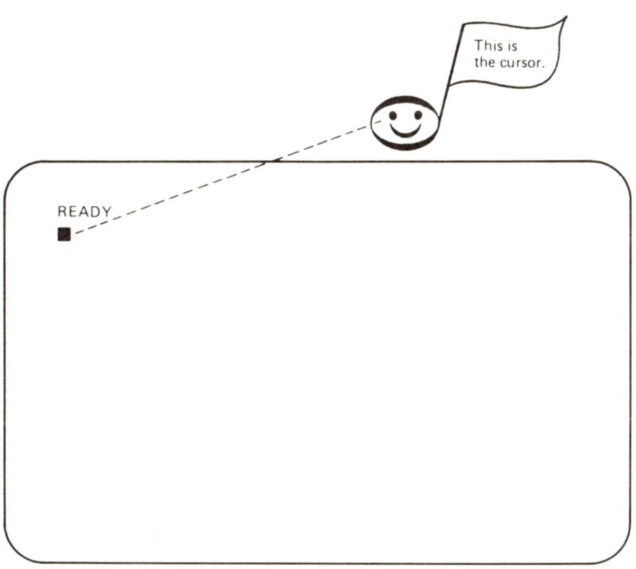

*Indicates trademark of Atari, Inc.

**This book does not try to tell you how to hook up the machine. That is explained very well in the *ATARI 400 or 800 Operators Manual* you received with your machine. It's easy to do, so we will assume your computer is "up and running."

You tell the computer what you want it to do by typing instructions, called commands.

The little square just below the word READY is called the cursor. As you type instructions, the cursor moves across the screen, so you'll know where the next letter will appear as you type it.

Before you begin, look at this diagram of the ATARI Computer's keyboard. Arrows point to two important keys (RETURN and SYSTEM RESET) you will learn to use in just a moment.

Now that you've looked over the keyboard, you're ready to give the machine a command. Type

```
SOUND Ø,121,1Ø,8
```

Be sure to type it exactly as you see it here. The computer is very particular about punctuation, so be sure to use a comma between numbers. It is also a very literal machine and is not able to guess what you mean; you must tell it exactly. Don't use substitutions such as the letter "o' for zero (Ø) or the letter "l" for the number 1, as you might on a conventional typewriter.

As you can see on your screen, the zeroes in the SOUND statement contain a slash mark (Ø), whereas the "o" in the SOUND does not. So remember that on the screen:

Ø is a zero
O is the letter "o"

What if, while typing your SOUND statement, you press a wrong number or spell "SUUND" or "SOUD," and realize you've made a mistake? It's easy to fix.

Just press the DELETE BACK S key near the upper right side of the

keyboard. This moves the cursor back (to the left) as many spaces as you want and erases the error. Then type the correct letters or numbers.

Okay, do you have a SOUND command that looks like this?

```
SOUND Ø,121,1Ø.,8
```

If you do, press the RETURN key and the machine will produce a single tone that is approximately the note middle C.

Can you hear it? Be sure the volume on your TV is turned up to a comfortable listening level.

The tone will stay on. To stop the tone type:

```
END
```

and press RETURN.

You can also stop it by pressing the SYSTEM RESET KEY (the yellow key at the upper right corner of the keyboard). When you do this, the sound stops and you see this again on the screen:

But what happens if you make a typing error in your SOUND statement and don't notice it? Suppose you put a period instead of a comma between 1Ø and 8, so it looks like this:

```
SOUND Ø,121,1Ø.8
```

If you do this and press the RETURN key, instead of a tone you'll get an ERROR message that looks something like this:

```
ERROR - SOUND Ø,121,1Ø.8
```

An ERROR Message is the machine's way of telling you it doesn't understand. Don't let an ERROR message upset you. The most advanced computer people get ERROR messages all the time. It only means that you have to find a different way to tell the machine what you want it to do.

Enough of ERRORS for the moment and back to the SOUND statement.

PARAMETERS

Each number separated by a comma in the SOUND statement can be changed to give the statement a different meaning. A number that affects the meaning of a statement is called a *parameter*. The SOUND statement in ATARI BASIC consists of four parameters.

Voice Parameter

The first parameter in the SOUND statement you've been using is the *voice parameter*. Your ATARI Computer has four voices, just like a barbershop quartet. ATARI BASIC counts voices a little differently from people though. It numbers its four voices Ø,1,2,3.

```
SOUND Ø,121,1Ø,1Ø
```

Voice 1 can play the same note like this:

```
SOUND 1,121,1Ø,1Ø
```

Now you type a SOUND statement for voices 2 and 3 to play the same note.

You'll get a chance to combine the voices with different notes soon, but for the moment let's stick with the first voice. That's voice Ø (zero) in the ATARI BASIC's SOUND statement.

Note Parameter

The second parameter in your SOUND statement is the *note parameter*. To get a feel for the note parameter, try this exercise:
First type:

```
SOUND Ø,243,1Ø,8
```

and press the RETURN key.

You should hear a nice low note played by the computer.
Now type:

```
SOUND Ø,6Ø,1Ø,8
```

and press the RETURN key.

Type END and press RETURN if you want to stop the sound.

By now you may have begun to realize that any time you give the computer a command, you must press the RETURN key to have the machine execute that command. So we'll stop telling you each time, although we will remind you occasionally.

Low numbers play high notes!
High numbers play low notes!

Using ATARI BASIC, you can play 256 different notes numbered from Ø to 255. When it comes to notes, not only does the computer start counting at zero, but it also counts backwards from the way we humans count. That is, it gives the highest notes the lowest numbers and the lowest notes the highest numbers. So 243 for the note parameter is a low note, while 26 is a high one.

Let's write a SOUND statement so the note parameter is a *variable* called N. That's simply a way of saying you can make N equal to different numbers, in this case numbers between Ø and 255 inclusive.

Now it looks like this:

```
SOUND Ø,N,1Ø,1Ø
```

(The letter "N" here represents a number. You may substitute a number from Ø to 255 for N in this SOUND statement.)

Try different numbers for the variable N to get a feeling for some of the notes that your ATARI Computer can generate. Remember to use the RETURN key after each new command!

Tone Parameter

The third parameter in the SOUND statement is the *tone parameter*. "Tone" here is different from the tone control on your radio. To get the idea of some possible "tones" you can produce, try this.

First go back to the original SOUND statement:

```
SOUND Ø,121,1Ø,1Ø
```

This makes a nice "pure" musical tone.

But you can make a sound something like a motorcycle cruising down the highway by simply changing the value of the tone parameter to 4 instead of 10. If you do that, the SOUND statement will look like this:

```
SOUND Ø,121,4,1Ø
```

You can make a variable out of the tone parameter in the same way you did with the note parameter. The statement would then take the following form:

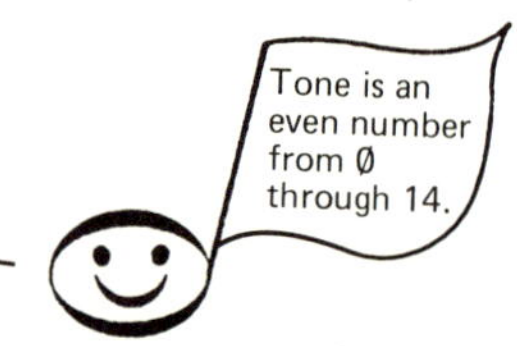


```
SOUND Ø,121,T,1Ø
```

There are eight possible "tones" available in ATARI BASIC, indicated by even numbers from Ø to 14. There's no particular reason for them being even numbers other than that's the way the machine was designed.

If you use an odd number like:

```
SOUND Ø,121,5,1Ø
```

it won't make a sound.

Note: Ø to 255
Tone: Ø,2,4,6,8,1Ø,12,14

Try different numbers for the variable "T" in the SOUND statement to see which ones you like. The values 1Ø and 14 should give you a very pure sounding tone. The other values give a variety of buzzing and scratching sounds. You'll explore these later when you get into creating sound effects.

Loudness Parameter

The final parameter in the SOUND statement is the *loudness parameter*. It has sixteen possible values, numbered from 0 to 15. The lowest value, which is 0, makes no sound. Later, you will see how this can be used as a way to turn off a note.

```
SOUND 0,121,10,L
```

The highest value of the loudness parameter is 15, the loudest tone. (Of course, all this depends on where you have the volume on your TV.)

First, try a value of 2 for "L" in this statement:

```
SOUND 0,121,10,2
```

Then, try 15 for "L":

```
SOUND 0,121,10,15
```

Now try a few more values of your own choice to get a feeling for the loudness parameter.

You have now explored all four parameters of the SOUND statement.

Here's a brief summary of what you've learned so far. This section may be helpful as a quick reference as you continue to explore on your own.

Defining each parameter as a variable, you can write the SOUND statement like this:

```
SOUND V,N,T,L*
```

V is for Voice . . . . Numbered 0 through 3.
  (Four voices—Zero is the first voice)
N is for Note . . . . Numbered 0 through 255.
  (0 is the highest pitch, 255 is the lowest)
T is for Tone . . . . Even numbers 0 through 14.
  (Odd numbers won't work—10 and 14 are "pure" tones)
L is for loudness . . . . . . Numbered 0 through 15.
  (0 is the quietest, 15 is the loudest)

*You can use any name you wish for these variables. For example, in the *ATARI 400/800 BASIC Reference Manual*, Pitch is used for the parameter we've called Note, Distortion is used for what we've called Tone, and Volume is used for the fourth parameter where we've used the name Loudness. Use whatever variable names you like.

COMBINING VOICES

Suppose you want to hear two voices together. To do this, type one SOUND statement for voice Ø, and then, without pressing SYSTEM RESET (but do press RETURN), type another statement for voice 1. For example, you might have:

```
SOUND Ø,121,1Ø,1Ø
SOUND 1,6Ø,1Ø,1Ø
```

Be sure the second statement is for voice 1 and not voice Ø again. This tells the machine to play middle C with the first voice and the note C an octave higher with the second voice. You can play up to four different voices at once in this way. You might have something like this:

```
SOUND Ø,121,1Ø,1Ø–(middle C)
SOUND 1,96,1Ø,1Ø–(the note E)
SOUND 2,81,1Ø,1Ø–(the note G)
SOUND 3,6Ø,1Ø,1Ø–(C one octave above middle C)
```

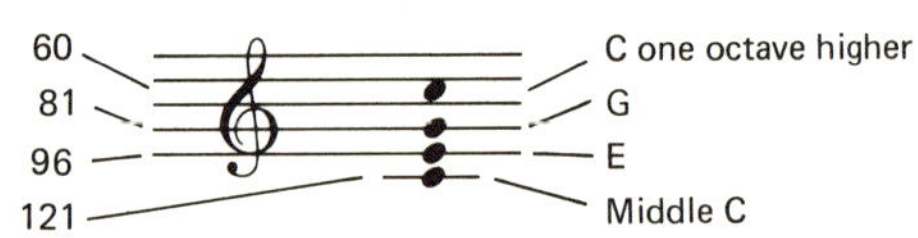

Remember, you can play any of 256 notes for the note variable. The following chart gives the number values for different notes in our western musical scale. You might want to make up some chords of your own before going on to the next section.

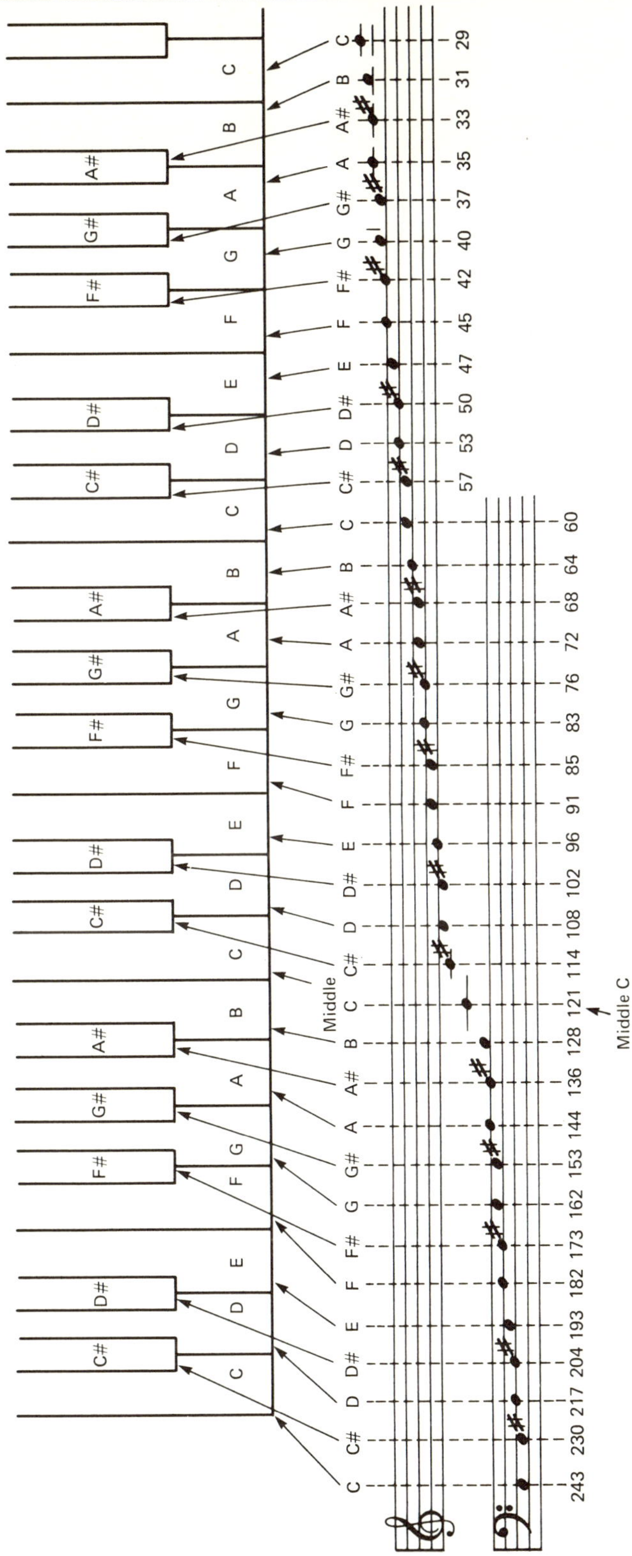
C 29
B 31
A# 33
A 35
G# 37
G 40
F# 42
F 45
E 47
D# 50
D 53
C# 57
C 60
B 64
A# 68
A 72
G# 76
G 83
F# 85
F 91
E 96
D# 102
D 108
C# 114
Middle C 121
B 128
A# 136
A 144
G# 153
G 162
F# 173
F 182
E 193
D# 204
D 217
C# 230
C 243
Middle C

EDITING

To change a parameter in the SOUND statement, you've learned to type the line over. For example, if you have:

```
SOUND Ø,121,1Ø,1Ø
```

You can change the note by typing:

```
SOUND Ø,243,1Ø,1Ø
```

But if you want to change just one part of a statement, for example the note parameter, your ATARI Computer has a special "editing" feature to make it easy.

First, look on the left side of the keyboard and find the control key that looks like this:

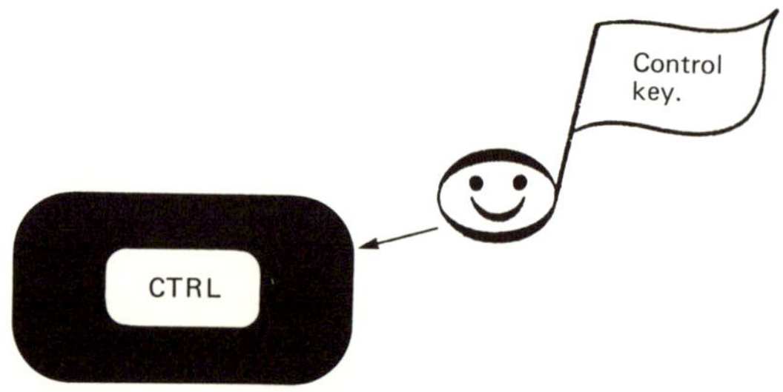

Got it?

Okay, now on the other side of the keyboard are four keys with little arrows on them. They look like this:

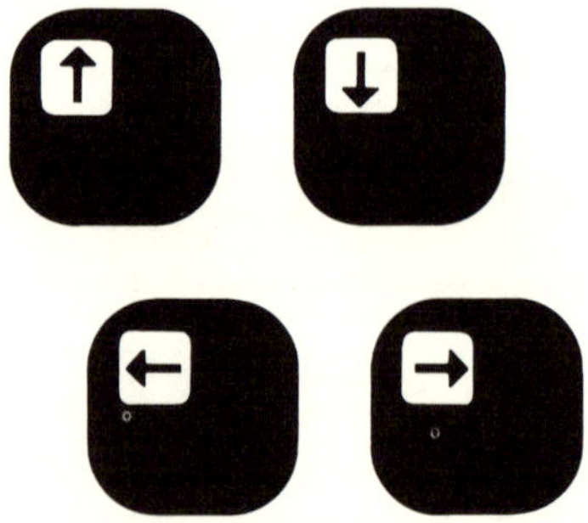

Now enter a SOUND statement like:

```
SOUND Ø,121,1Ø,1Ø
```

Once you've done that, hold down the control key, CTRL with one hand and while still holding it down, press the key with the arrow pointing up [↑] . When you do this, the cursor will move towards the top of the screen.

Try to move it up until it covers the S in the SOUND statement. If the cursor goes past the S, don't worry about it. There's another key with the arrow pointing down [↓] .

Sure enough! you just have to hold the CTRL key and press the key with the arrow pointing down to make the cursor go the other way.

You've probably guessed by now that the other two keys [←] and [→] make the cursor move back and forth across the screen. Be sure to hold the CTRL key down when you do it, though! Now, try to move the cursor around with these keys until it is over the 2 in the note parameter of the SOUND statement:

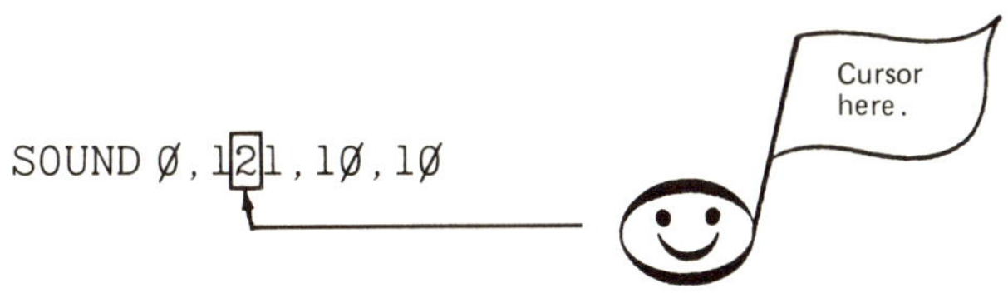

Once you've got that, type a 9 and press RETURN. Now you get:

```
SOUND Ø,191,1Ø,1Ø
```

If you do this while the SOUND statement is playing, the note will change. You can practice this editing feature and also explore the sounds made by different values for the parameters of the SOUND statement, as demonstrated below.

This kind of editing takes a while to get the hang of, so don't be too discouraged if everything didn't work for you the first time you tried it.

If you do have problems, it might help to just practice moving the cursor around first and then use it to change the parameters in a SOUND statement.

Exploring SOUND Parameters

Once you've gotten the idea of editing by moving the cursor around, try this experiment.

First enter:

```
SOUND Ø,121,1Ø,1Ø
SOUND 1,96,1Ø,1Ø
SOUND 2,81,1Ø,1Ø
SOUND 3,6Ø,1Ø,1Ø
```

Now while the chord is playing, move the cursor up and change any parameter in any SOUND statement you want. As soon as you change a number and press RETURN, a new sound will occur.

For example, put the cursor over the 9 in the note parameter for voice 1 and change it to 2. Or change the tone parameter to 6 in voice 3, and so on.

Have fun exploring!

In this chapter you've learned to make some different sounds with your Atari computer. In the next chapter you will learn some graphics commands that will allow you to draw figures and put colors on the screen.

Self-Test

Complete the following Self-Test to see what you already can do with your computer.

1. Using the note chart in Figure 1 on page 9, see if you can play the note C# above middle C in the following SOUND statement:

```
SOUND Ø,N,1Ø,1Ø
```

2. Now play the highest A that you can play.
3. Now play a very quiet note with the loudness parameter.
4. Now play a loud note.
5. The notes of a G major chord are G–B–D. See if you can enter three SOUND statements to play the notes of this chord.

Answers

1. SOUND Ø,114,1Ø,1Ø
2. SOUND Ø,35,1Ø,1Ø
3. Something like:

```
SOUND Ø,121,1Ø,2
```

4. Something like:

```
SOUND Ø,121,1Ø,15
```

5. You can use any of the values for the notes G–B–D in the note chart. You need to use three different voices.

   Example:

```
G    SOUND Ø,81,1Ø,1Ø
D    SOUND 1,1Ø8,1Ø,1Ø
B    SOUND 2,64,1Ø,1Ø
```

CHAPTER TWO

Picture Yourself Doing Graphics

To create graphics with your ATARI Computer, use a graphics mode. Several graphics modes allow you to do various things. A good one to start with is graphics mode 3.

GRAPHICS MODE 3

The command you need to enter graphics mode 3 is:

```
GRAPHICS 3
```

or

```
GR. 3
```

If you use the short version, be sure to include the period. When you type this graphics command and press the RETURN key, the screen changes to look like this:

The area at the bottom of the screen with the word READY and the cursor is called the *text window*. It displays written information (text).

Use the rest of the screen for creating graphics. To do this, you tell the machine to use a color—even if your TV is black and white.

Type:

```
COLOR 1
```

and press RETURN.

Be sure NOT to press the SYSTEM RESET key after each command or you'll have to start over. When you ENTER this command (by typing it and pressing RETURN), you'll see what you've typed displayed in the text window, along with READY and the cursor. The machine is waiting for another command.

Plotting a Point

Let's plot a point. The PLOT command looks like this:

```
PLOT 1Ø,5
```

Try entering PLOT 1Ø,5 and see what happens. You should end up with a screen that looks like this:

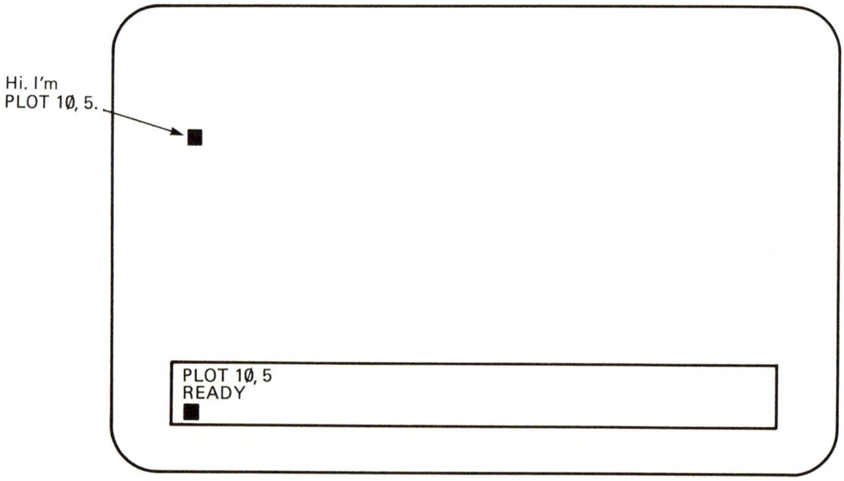

This dot should be orange. Adjust the color on your TV until the dot is orange.

Do you see a little square on the screen?

By now you may be saying to yourself, "That's great, but what does . . .

```
PLOT 1Ø,5
```

really mean?"

Well . . .

When you ENTER a graphics mode, the computer divides the screen into a number of columns and rows, something like this:

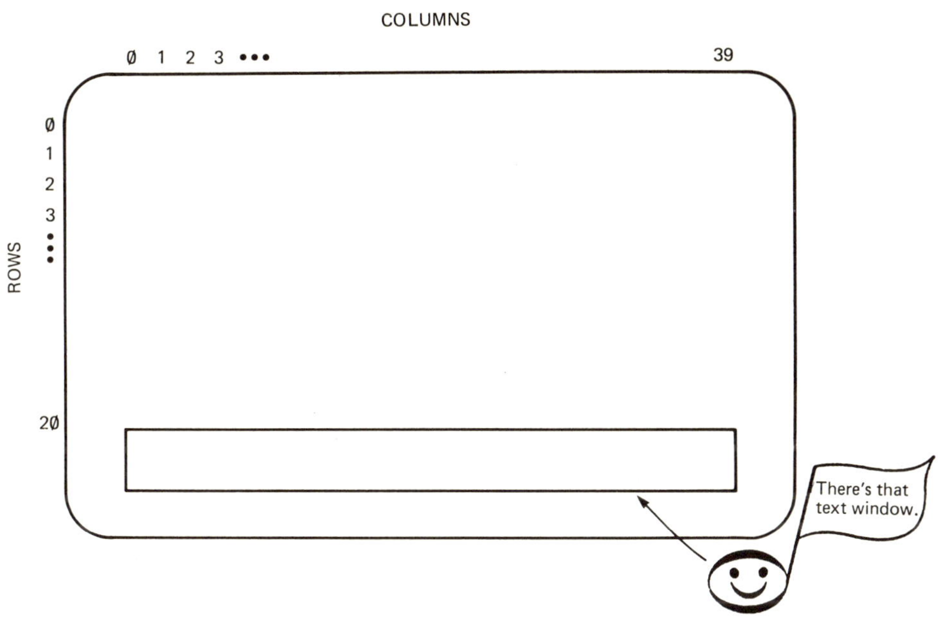

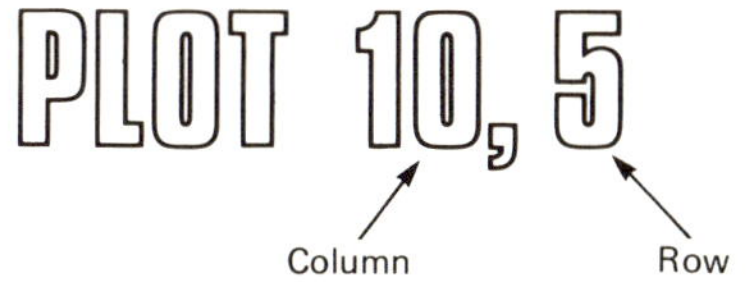

The first number in the PLOT statement tells the computer in which column to plot the point. The second number tells it in which row to plot the point. You've told the machine to plot a point in column 1Ø, row 5.

Graphics mode 3 has 4Ø columns (numbered Ø through 39) and 2Ø rows (numbered Ø through 19).

In graphics mode 3 (GRAPHICS 3 or GR. 3):

Columns (Ø–39)
Rows (Ø–19)

Okay, now plot these points:

```
PLOT Ø,Ø
PLOT 39,Ø
PLOT 39,19
PLOT Ø,19
```

Now type:

```
COLOR 2
```

and then:

```
PLOT 1,Ø
```

You should get a light green dot in the upper left corner now:

See if you can plot another point using:

```
COLOR 3
```

It will be dark blue.
Now type:

```
COLOR Ø
```

and press RETURN.
Then type:

```
PLOT 39,Ø
```

The dot in the upper right corner disappears:

COLOR Ø plots a point in the same color as the background screen, so you can use it to *erase* a point you've already plotted.

Colors

The following chart shows the different colors for plot points on the screen in graphics mode 3 using values of Ø through 3 for the COLOR command:

COLOR Ø—Background Screen
COLOR 1—Orange
COLOR 2—Light Green
COLOR 3—Dark Blue

In Chapter 7 you'll learn to put several more colors on the screen as you learn to use the SETCOLOR command.

Try plotting a few more points on your own to get the idea. Then press the SYSTEM RESET key to clear the screen.

Drawing a Line

Another GRAPHICS command! Use DRAWTO to draw lines. Before you use this command, you must plot a point.

Do the following very carefully.

First type:

```
GRAPHICS 3      and press RETURN
```

Now type:

```
COLOR 1      and press RETURN
```

Then, plot a point by typing:

```
PLOT 1Ø,5      (You got it! Press RETURN)
```

Now you get to draw a line. Let's say you want to draw the line over to column 3Ø, row 5. You use a

DRAWTO statement

to draw a line from a point you've just plotted to another point on the screen.

To do this, just type:

```
DRAWTO 3Ø,5
```

Be sure to type DRAWTO as one word or the computer won't understand. (Try DRAW TO and draw an ERROR message).

When you type this command and press RETURN, you'll get a screen display that looks like this:

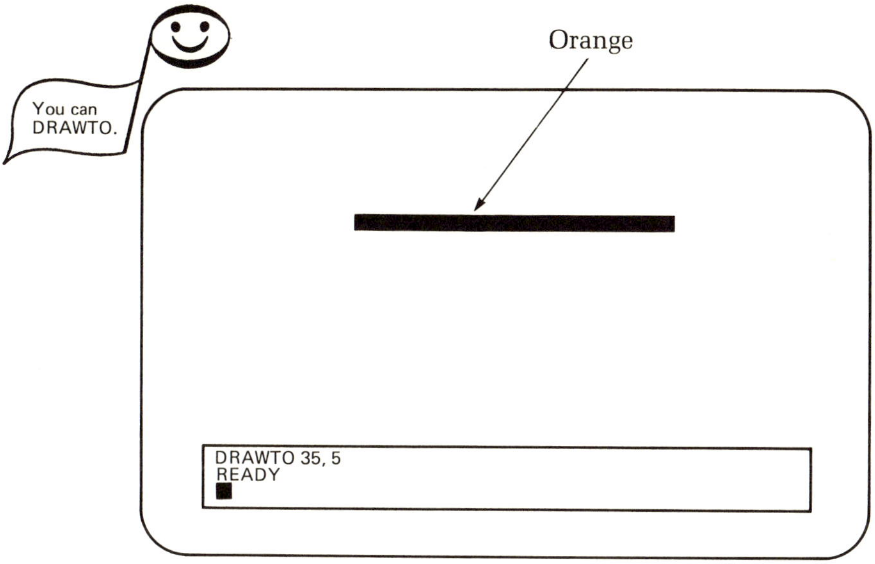

The computer draws a line from column 1Ø, row 5 to column 3Ø, row 5.

Staircase

Horizontal and vertical lines will be straight, but lines drawn at an angle will have a staircase effect in graphics mode 3. To see this staircase effect, push the SYSTEM RESET key to start over again.

Now ENTER:

```
GR. 3
```

and then:

```
COLOR 2
```

then:

```
PLOT Ø,Ø
```

and finally:

```
DRAWTO 39,19
```

If you entered everything correctly, you should get this on the screen:

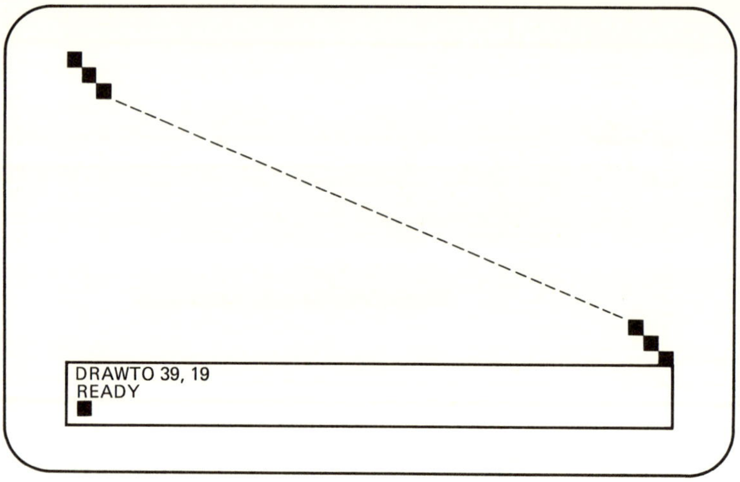

The text window will show the last command you've typed, the word READY, and the cursor.

Drawing a Figure

Let's draw a new figure on the screen. First clear the screen by pressing SYSTEM RESET.
Now type:

```
GRAPHICS 3
```

then:

```
COLOR 1
```

and:

```
PLOT 1Ø,8
```

Now add the following DRAWTO commands:

```
DRAWTO 2Ø,8
DRAWTO 1Ø,18
DRAWTO 15,3
DRAWTO 2Ø,18
DRAWTO 1Ø,8
```

By the time you finish, you should have a figure that looks like this:

Changing the Line Colors

You can draw different colored lines in the same way you plotted different colored points. If you still have the figure on the screen, type:

```
COLOR 2
```

and press RETURN.
Then type:

```
DRAWTO 2Ø,8
```

The horizontal line will turn:

Can you color the next line dark blue? Hint: COLOR 3 is dark blue.
Try experimenting a bit on your own to get a feeling for PLOT statements and DRAWTO statements.

GRAPHICS MODE 4

Okay, let's have a look at another graphics mode. Graphics mode 4 fills the screen with 8Ø columns and 4Ø rows numbered as follows:

Columns (Ø–79)
Rows (Ø–39)

To fill the same amount of screen space with twice as many columns and rows, the computer must plot smaller points.
To see this, ENTER:

```
GR. 4
```

then:

```
COLOR 1
```

and then:

```
PLOT 1Ø,8
```

Now, you should see a much smaller dot on the screen than you saw using graphics mode 3.

ENTER the same DRAWTO commands you used for the figure in graphics mode 3. You should end up with the same figure, but it will be smaller and will be located in the upper left on the screen.

GRAPHICS MODE 6

Now let's try graphics mode 6, which has even more columns and rows, and plots even smaller dots.
First press the SYSTEM RESET, and then ENTER:

```
GR. 6
```

and then:

```
COLOR 1
```

Now ENTER:

```
PLOT 5Ø,3Ø
```

Pretty small dots this time!!
Now without pressing SYSTEM RESET, let's add some more commands.
First ENTER:

```
DRAWTO 8Ø,15
```

then:

```
DRAWTO 11Ø,3Ø
```

and finally:

```
DRAWTO 5Ø,3Ø
```

Be sure to press RETURN after each new statement you type. What did you get? Did you get a triangle? If you did, that's great! If you didn't, try it again and see what happens.

Before you clear the screen, try adding:

```
DRAWTO 8Ø,45
DRAWTO 11Ø,3Ø
DRAWTO 8Ø,55
DRAWTO 8Ø,5
DRAWTO 5Ø,3Ø
```

Did you get a figure like this?

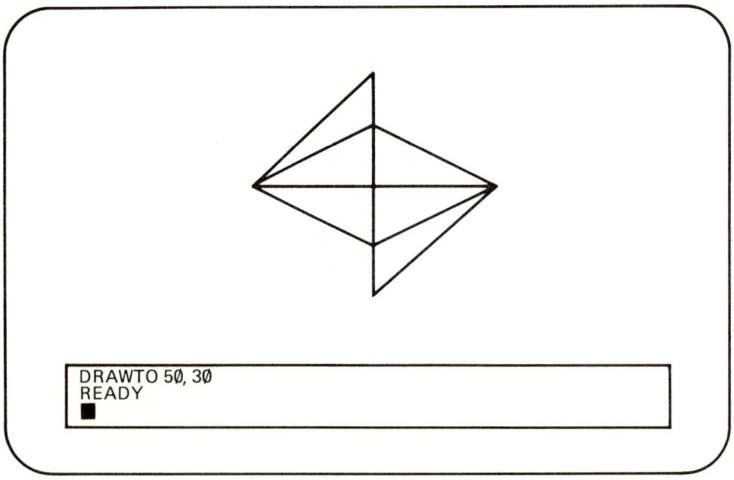

The following chart shows the number of columns and rows in several different graphics modes available in ATARI BASIC.

Mode Number	Number of Columns	Graphic Positions Rows	Text Window
3	40	20	4 lines
4,5	80	40	4 lines
6,7	158	80	4 lines

Although some graphics modes have the same number of columns and rows, the colors they are able to make are different. These differences depend upon some other commands which you have not yet learned.

In Chapter 7 you will learn about the SETCOLOR command which enables you to create a variety of colors for the figure, the background screen, and the text window.

Self-Test

1. What does the PLOT statement tell the computer to do?
2. Plot a point in column 12, row 1Ø of graphics mode 4.
3. Now draw a line from that point to column 12, row 3Ø.
4. Which graphics mode provides the largest number of positions for plotting points?
5. What COLOR command will erase a dot by coloring it the same as the background screen?
6. What statement would you enter to complete a square after entering the following statements:

```
GRAPHICS 7
COLOR 2
PLOT 35,1Ø
DRAWTO 55,1Ø
DRAWTO 55,3Ø
DRAWTO 35,1Ø
```

____

Answers

1. It tells the computer to plot a point in a specific column and row.
2. ENTER the following commands and press RETURN after each line:

```
GR. 4
COLOR 1
PLOT 12,1Ø
```

3. Add this command:

```
DRAWTO 12,3Ø
```

4. Graphics modes 6 and 7.
5. COLOR Ø
6. DRAWTO 35,5

Challenges

1. Draw two separate triangles on the screen in graphics mode 6.
2. Draw the last figure in this chapter but make each line a different color.
3. Draw "Please Note" on the screen.

CHAPTER THREE

A Graphics Program

DIRECT COMMANDS vs PROGRAMS

The instructions you've been giving the computer are called *direct commands*. This simply means the machine executes the command right away or "directly." The computer doesn't remember direct commands, so if you want it to do the same thing again, you have to type the instruction again.

Frequently, you will want to give the machine an instruction it can remember and use later. A set of this kind of instructions is called a *program*.

To make sure your computer doesn't already have some information in its memory, there are a few things to do whenever starting a new program.

First, press the SYSTEM RESET key.
Now type the word NEW and press RETURN.

You're ready to start your program. To write a program, use the same commands you've learned so far. But now, you give each command a *line number* as you type it.

For example, you would write a graphics program to plot a point like this:
First type:

```
1Ø GR. 3
```

and press RETURN. What happens?

"Nothing happened," you say.

Actually, something has happened. The machine has remembered the instruction.

Now type:

```
2Ø COLOR 1
```

Next type:

```
30 PLOT 10,5
```

And finally:

```
40 END
```

Always press the RETURN key after you type each line of a program. In this way the command indicated in that line is entered into the computer's memory.

Remember, if you make a mistake in typing, you can use your editing keys to correct it.

LISTING A PROGRAM

If you've typed each command correctly and pressed RETURN after each command, there should be a program in the computer's memory. Let's make sure it's all there:

First press SYSTEM RESET.
Then type:

```
LIST
```

and press RETURN.
You should get this on the screen:

```
10 GRAPHICS 3
20 COLOR 1
30 PLOT 10,5
40 END
```

Make sure your listing is the same as this.

RUNNING A PROGRAM

So how do you make it work?
Just type:

```
RUN
```

and press RETURN.

When you RUN the program, the computer plots the point for you.

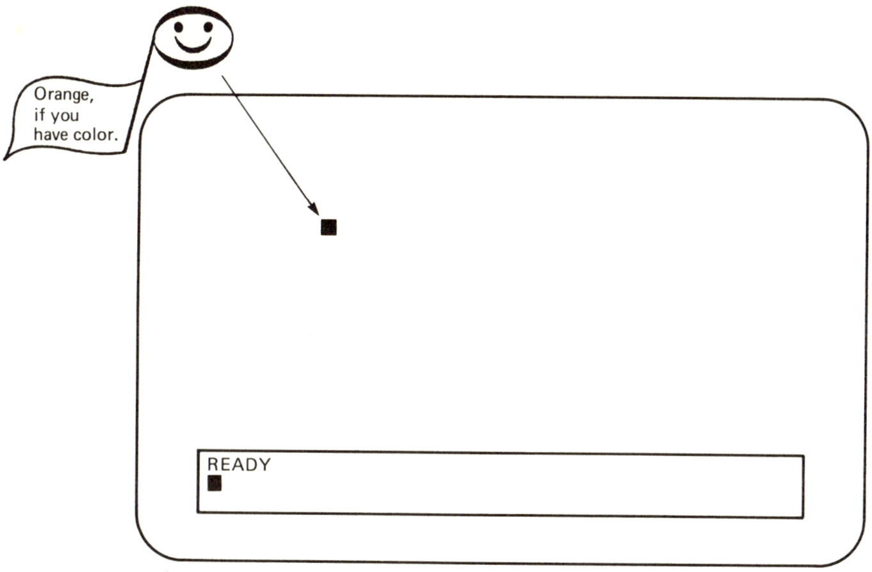

Remember what happened when you were using direct commands? Every time you pressed the SYSTEM RESET key, you had to type the instructions to plot a point or make a sound from the beginning again. But the computer remembers a program, so you can RUN it again. To see this happen, first press SYSTEM RESET.

Now type:

```
RUN
```

And press RETURN.

Your program RUNs again!

So . . . once a program is in the computer's memory, it can be RUN over and over until you erase it by typing NEW and pressing RETURN.

Turning the machine off will also erase a program from its memory.

ADDING TO A PROGRAM

You might have wondered, "Does the computer only understand line numbers in multiples of 1Ø (that is 1Ø, 2Ø, 3Ø. . . .)?"

The answer is no. However, it's a good idea to leave some space between commands in case you want to add more instructions later.

Suppose, for example, you want to plot another point before the end of the program. First, you'll want to have a look at your program again.

To do this, press SYSTEM RESET and then type:

```
LIST
```

Now when you press RETURN, your program is shown on the screen again.

```
1Ø GRAPHICS 3
2Ø COLOR 1
3Ø PLOT 1Ø,5
4Ø END
```

Okay, now try adding:

```
35 PLOT 14,4
```

and press RETURN.

If you LIST the program again (by typing LIST and pressing RETURN), you'll see that the computer, being the orderly machine that it is, has put line 35 in sequence between 3Ø and 4Ø.

```
1Ø GRAPHICS 3
2Ø COLOR 1
3Ø PLOT 1Ø,5
35 PLOT 14,4
4Ø END
```

When you RUN this program (by typing RUN and pressing RETURN), you get two dots.

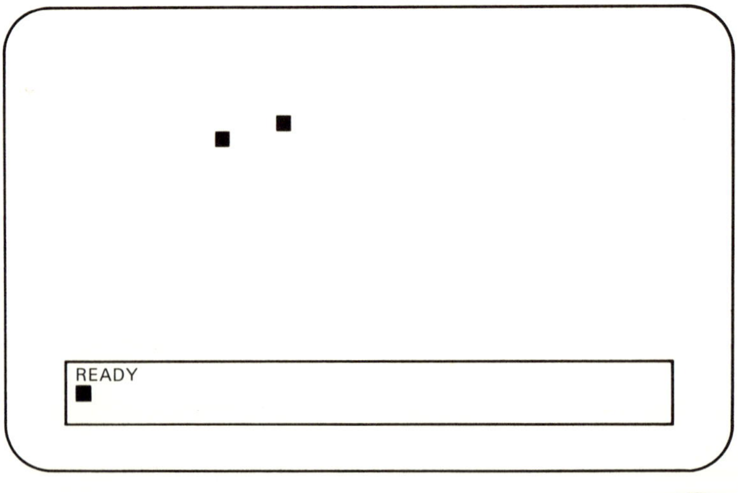

You might decide you want the computer to draw a verticle line before plotting 14, 4. Easy enough, just add another line, something like:

```
32 DRAWTO 1Ø,1Ø
```

When you type the RUN command and press RETURN to execute this program, it will look like this:

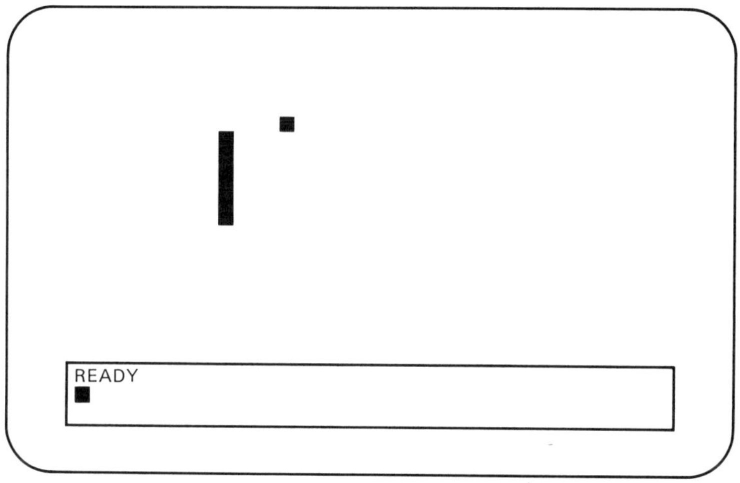

Care to RUN it again? Give it a try!

Now press SYSTEM RESET to clear the screen and use the LIST command to have a look at your program. Your listing should read like this:

```
1Ø GRAPHICS 3
2Ø COLOR 1
3Ø PLOT 1Ø,5
32 DRAWTO 1Ø,1Ø
35 PLOT 14,4
4Ø END
```

When you RUN a program, the computer will execute each line of the program in sequence. By leaving some space in the original line numbers, you can add instructions to this sequence as you go along.

CHANGE COLORS

Let's make the dot light green. Just add:

```
34 COLOR 2
```

LIST the program again. It should be:

```
10 GRAPHICS 3
20 COLOR 1
30 PLOT 10,5
32 DRAWTO 10,10
34 COLOR 2
35 PLOT 14,4
40 END
```

Try adding another color (0–3) and a few DRAWTO statements of your own between lines 35 and 40.

REM STATEMENTS

As programs begin to get longer and more involved, you'll need ways to keep track of what you are doing. A useful tool for marking different parts of a program is the REM statement. The REM statement does not affect how the program runs. To see this, ENTER the following short program and then RUN it.

```
10 GRAPHICS 3
20 COLOR 1
30 PLOT 5,5
110 DRAWTO 30,5
```

You should get an orange line on the screen like this:

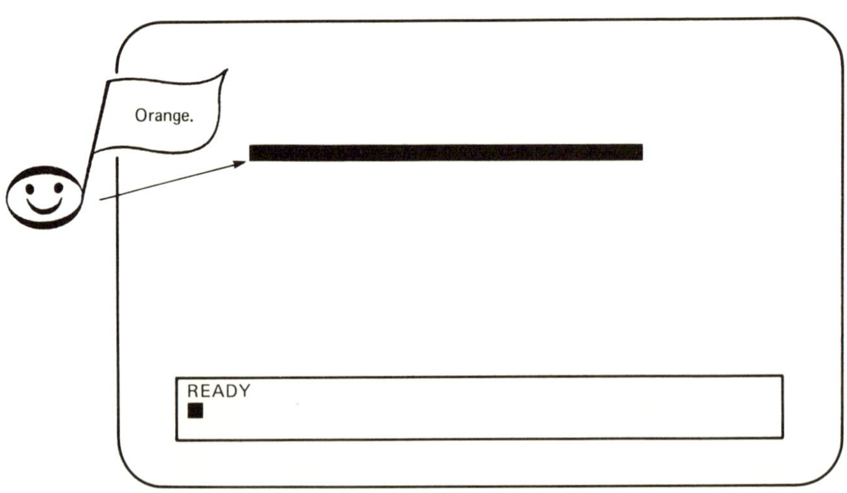

Now LIST the program. It should be:

```
1Ø GRAPHICS 3
2Ø COLOR 1
3Ø PLOT 5,5
11Ø DRAWTO 3Ø,5
```

Now add this REM statement:

```
1ØØ REM ** ORANGE LINE
```

Now RUN the program again. It should work exactly as it did before. We're going to add more lines to draw a figure, so let's put another REM statement in the program to mark the starting point of the drawing.

```
25 REM ** STARTING POINT
```

The listing now looks like this:

```
1Ø GRAPHICS 3
2Ø COLOR 1
25 REM ** STARTING POINT
3Ø PLOT 5,5
1ØØ REM ** ORANGE LINE
11Ø DRAWTO 3Ø,5
```

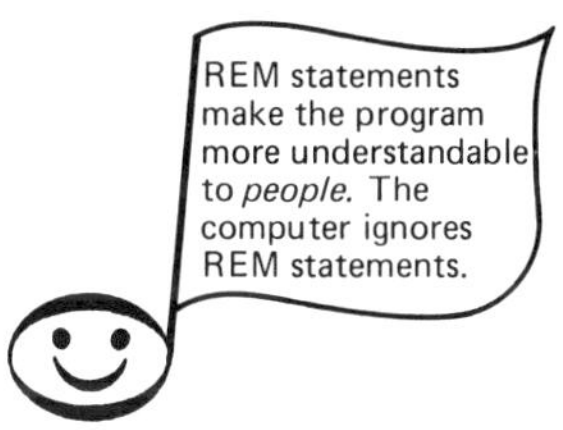

But it still runs the same. Try it and see.

BUILDING BLOCKS

It is very helpful to build programs in "blocks" with REM statements to explain different parts of the program. That's why we skipped to line 1ØØ for:

```
1ØØ REM ** ORANGE LINE
11Ø DRAWTO 3Ø,5
```

Let's add another block with a blue line. ENTER these lines:

```
2ØØ REM ** BLUE LINE
21Ø COLOR 3
22Ø DRAWTO 5,15
```

Make sure this is what you have for a complete listing:

```
10 GRAPHICS 3
20 COLOR 1
25 REM ** STARTING POINT
30 PLOT 5,5
100 REM ** ORANGE LINE
110 DRAWTO 30,5
200 REM ** BLUE LINE
210 COLOR 3
220 DRAWTO 5,15
```

Then RUN the program and this should appear on the screen:

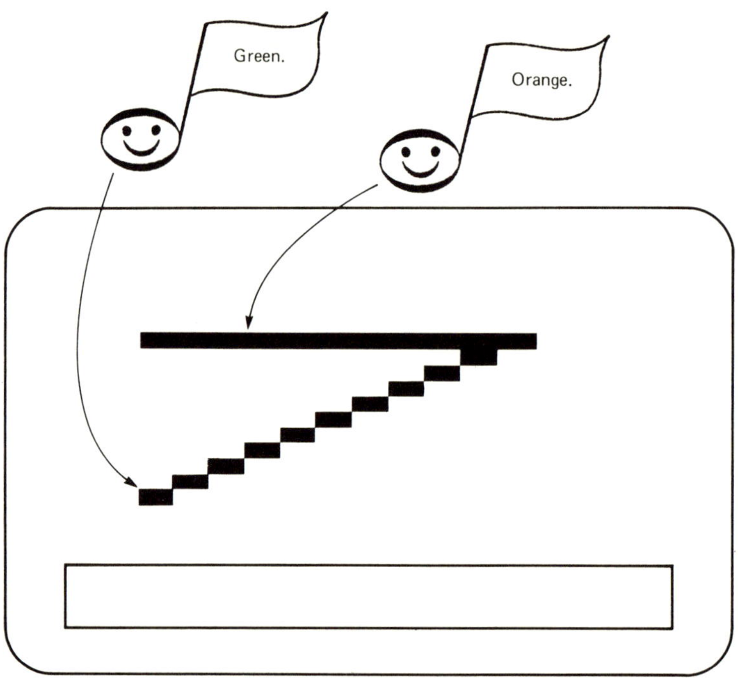

Now, add the following blocks to the program:

```
300 REM ** GREEN LINE
310 COLOR 2
320 DRAWTO 30,15
400 REM ** BLUE LINE
410 COLOR 3
420 DRAWTO 5,5
500 REM ** THAT'S ALL FOLKS
510 END
```

The program should now look like this when you RUN it:

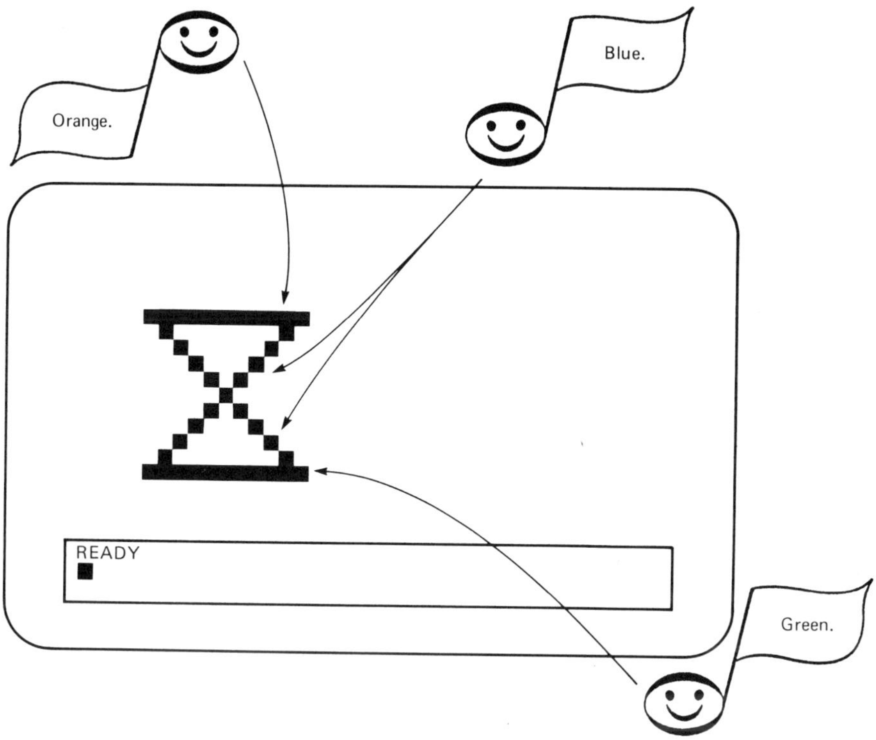

Here's the complete listing:

```
10 GRAPHICS 3
20 COLOR 1
25 REM ** STARTING POINT
30 PLOT 5,5

100 REM ** ORANGE LINE
110 DRAWTO 30,5

200 REM ** BLUE LINE
210 COLOR 3
220 DRAWTO 5,15

300 REM ** GREEN LINE
310 COLOR 2
320 DRAWTO 30,15

400 REM ** BLUE LINE
410 COLOR 3
420 DRAWTO 5,5

500 REM ** THAT'S ALL FOLKS
510 END
```

Try to add some different colored lines of your own.

DRAW A CUBE

We're going to give you a program listing to draw a cube on the screen. ENTER each block of the program and occasionally RUN it before you enter the next block. For example, RUN it after line 240 and then after line 350, and so on. Save the listing for the exercises that follow.

Here's the listing:

```
1 REM *** COLOR CUBE
1Ø GRAPHICS 5
2Ø COLOR 1

1ØØ REM ** STARTING POINT
11Ø PLOT 2Ø,15

2ØØ REM ** TOP OF CUBE
21Ø DRAWTO 3Ø,1Ø
22Ø DRAWTO 4Ø,15
23Ø DRAWTO 3Ø,2Ø
24Ø DRAWTO 2Ø,15

3ØØ REM ** THE SIDES
31Ø COLOR 2
32Ø DRAWTO 2Ø,25
33Ø DRAWTO 3Ø,3Ø
34Ø DRAWTO 4Ø,25
35Ø DRAWTO 4Ø,15

4ØØ REM ** FRONT LINE
41Ø PLOT 3Ø,2Ø
42Ø DRAWTO 3Ø,3Ø

5ØØ END
```

Here's what happens. First you get:

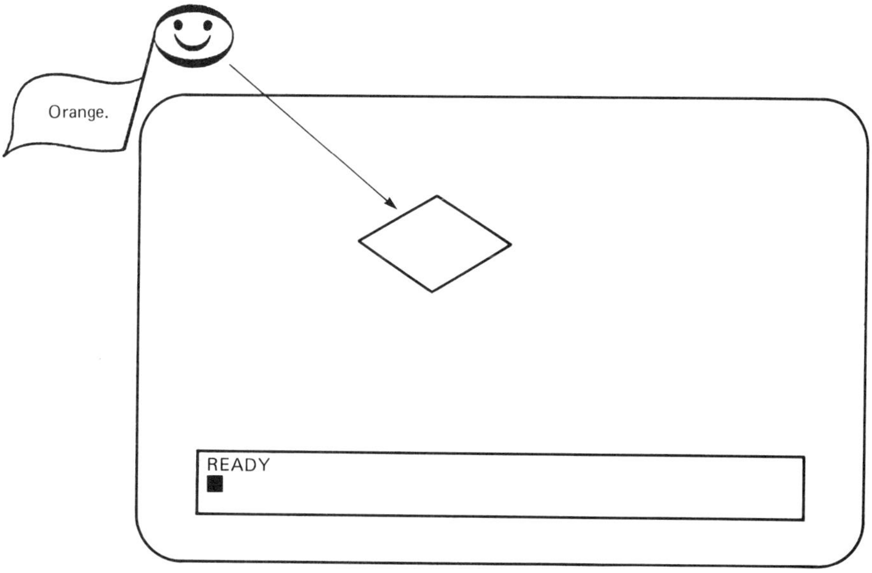

And then you get:

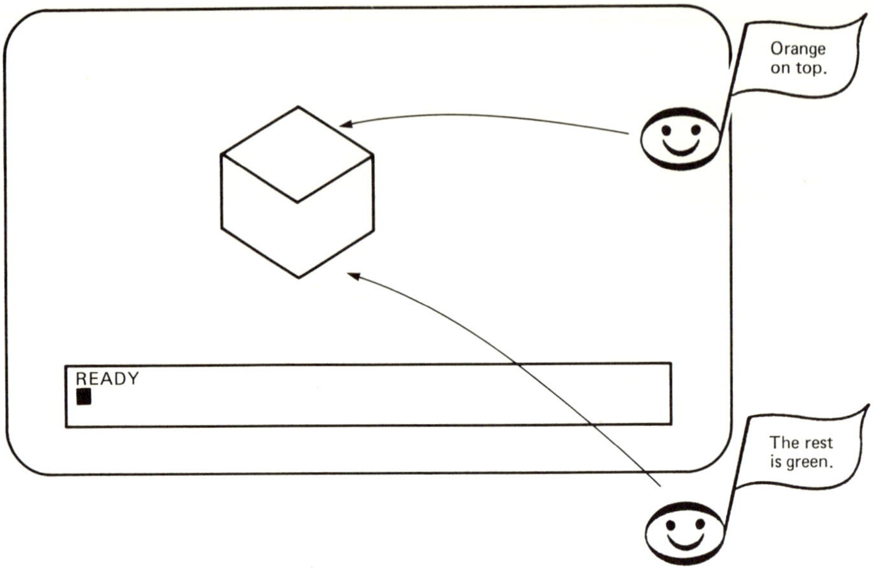

And finally:

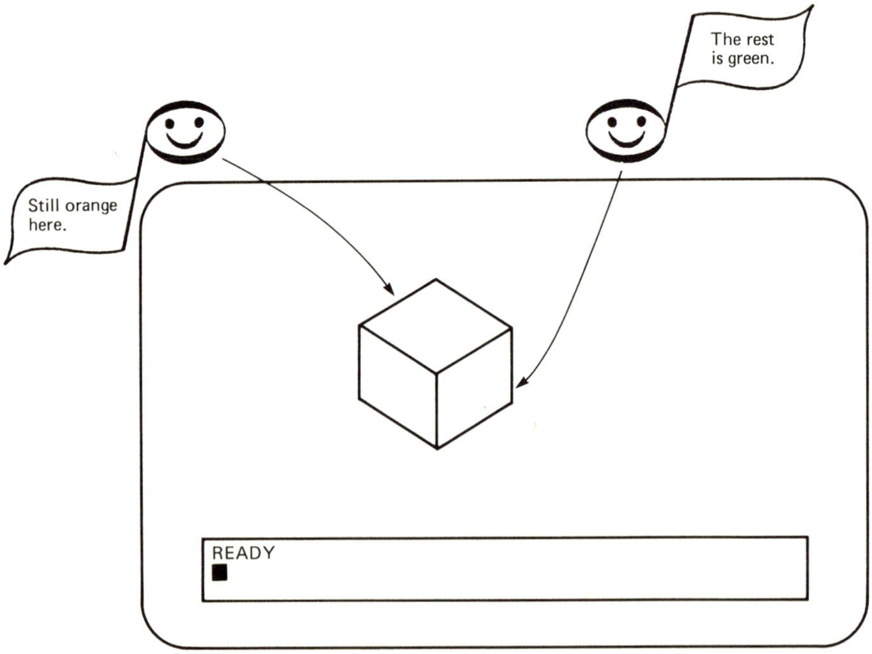

In Chapter 7 you will learn to use a much greater variety of colors for both the figures you draw and the background screen. This is done with the SETCOLOR command, but you need to learn a few more programming tools to easily understand this command.

In the next chapter you will learn to combine sound and graphics.

Self-Test

1. What do you call a set of instructions (with line numbers) that tells the computer what you want it to do?
2. How would you store this command in the computer's memory?

```
GRAPHICS 3
```

3. Why do you use line numbers like 1Ø, 2Ø, 3Ø instead of 1, 2, 3?
4. Will the "Color Cube" program run differently if you take out line 2ØØ?
5. Why won't the "Color Cube" program run using graphics mode 3?

Answers

1. A program
2. Give it a line number and press RETURN. For example:

```
2Ø GRAPHICS 3
```

3. To leave space to add more lines later
4. No. REM statements don't change the way a program runs.
5. Because graphics mode 3 has columns Ø through 39 and rows Ø through 19, and the dimensions of the cube go beyond that.

Challenges

1. Run the "Color Cube" program in graphics mode 7.
2. Plot some more points.
3. Add some DRAWTO statements.
4. See if you can write a program that will draw the figure at the end of Chapter 2.

CHAPTER FOUR

Sound And Graphics Together

So far you have learned to make some sounds and also to create some graphics with your ATARI Computer. In this chapter you will learn to make sound and graphics together. You will also learn an easy way to make the computer play a melody with READ and DATA statements.

Let's start with a graphics program using some of the things you learned in the last chapter:

```
1 REM *** SOUND AND COLOR
1Ø GRAPHICS 3
2Ø COLOR 1
3Ø PLOT 1Ø,1Ø
```

when you ENTER this correctly and RUN it, the machine plots a point in column 1Ø, row 1Ø.

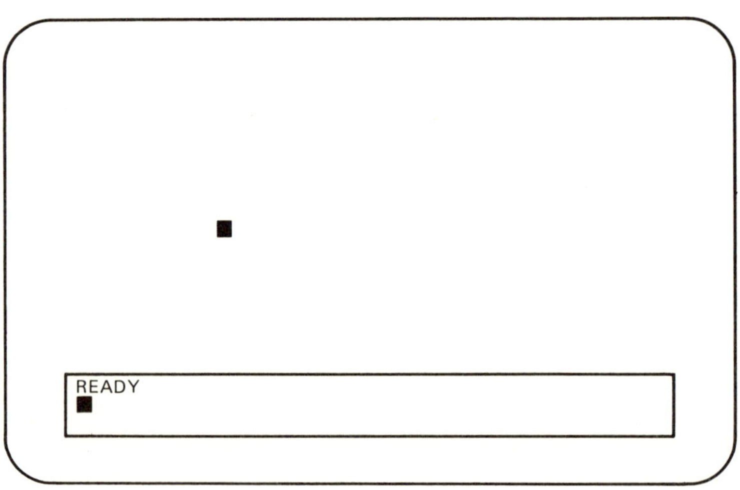

To add a SOUND statement, press SYSTEM RESET, then LIST the program. Now add:

```
2ØØ REM ** VOICE Ø PLAYS MIDDLE C
21Ø SOUND Ø,121,1Ø,1Ø
```

When you RUN the program, you don't hear the voice! What happened?

Well, the machine executed line 21Ø so fast you didn't hear the note played. It then finished the program and printed READY in the text window. To stay in the program, the machine must be given a command like this:

```
3ØØ REM ** VOICE STAYS ON
31Ø GOTO 21Ø
```

310 GOTO 210

The listing of the program now looks like this:

```
1 REM *** SOUND AND GRAPHICS
1Ø GRAPHICS 3
2Ø COLOR 1
3Ø PLOT 1Ø,15

2ØØ REM ** VOICE Ø PLAYS MIDDLE C
21Ø SOUND Ø,121,1Ø,1Ø

Optional→ 3ØØ REM ** VOICE STAYS ON
31Ø GOTO 21Ø
```

Now when you RUN the program, it puts a dot on the screen and you hear a continuous single tone, the note middle C. (You don't have to include the REM statements. The program will RUN the same without them.)

When the machine gets to line 31Ø, the GOTO statement tells it to go back to line 21Ø and play the note again. It keeps doing this (thus forming a "loop") until you press the SYSTEM RESET key to stop the RUN.

The machine executes the loop in lines 21Ø and 31Ø so fast that you hear it as a single tone, even though it's actually playing the note over and over.

FOR-NEXT LOOPS

Instead of having voice Ø stay on, suppose you want to have it play for a while and then turn it off.

Since the computer does things so fast, it is sometimes necessary to tell it to *pause* before going on.

You do this by telling it to count to itself for a while. The machine counts by using a:

```
FOR-NEXT loop
```

You want the computer to pause after it plays the note, so put the FOR-NEXT loop after line 21Ø.

It will look like this:

```
3ØØ REM ** PAUSE-NOTE ON
31Ø FOR P=1 TO 5ØØ
32Ø NEXT P
```

When you ENTER these lines (by typing each one and pressing RETURN), they will replace the previous lines 3ØØ and 31Ø. The FOR-NEXT loop in lines 31Ø and 32Ø is now telling the computer to count to 5ØØ.

Your complete program listing now looks like this:

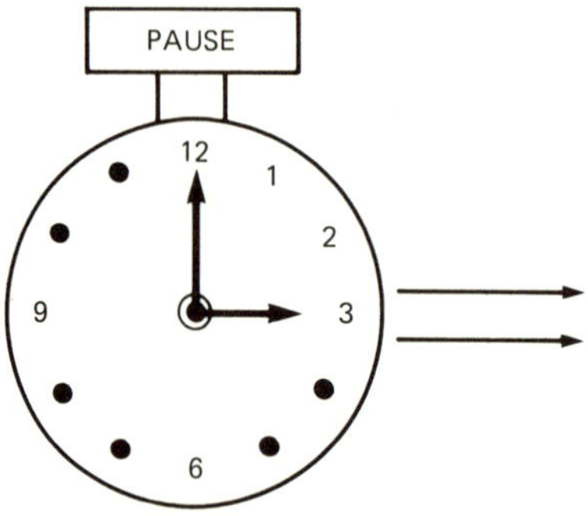


```
1 REM *** SOUND AND COLOR
1Ø GRAPHICS 3
2Ø COLOR 1
3Ø PLOT 1Ø,1Ø

2ØØ REM ** VOICE Ø PLAYS MIDDLE C
21Ø SOUND Ø,121,1Ø,1Ø

3ØØ REM ** PAUSE-NOTE ON
31Ø FOR P=1 TO 5ØØ
32Ø NEXT P
```

The spaces make it easier for you to read the program. They won't show up that way in your listing.

Now RUN the program. The dot should appear on the screen. The note plays for a while and then turns off. When the note stops playing, the word READY appears again in the text window.

The note stays on for as long as it takes the machine to count to 500 in lines 310 and 320. Not long, is it?

Let's try changing the amount of time it pauses to make the note stay on a little longer.

First, change line 310 to:

```
310 FOR P=1 TO 1000
```

To do this just type the new line 310 and press RETURN.

Now when you RUN the program, it should put the dot on the screen and then play the note for a longer time.

Try changing line 310 to play some very fast notes and then some much longer ones. Then change it back to:

```
310 FOR P=1 TO 500
```

The complete listing is back to:

```
1 REM *** SOUND AND COLOR
1Ø GRAPHICS 3
2Ø COLOR 1
3Ø PLOT 1Ø,1Ø

2ØØ REM ** VOICE Ø PLAYS MIDDLE C
21Ø SOUND Ø,121,1Ø,1Ø

3ØØ REM ** PAUSE—NOTE ON
31Ø FOR P=1 TO 5ØØ
32Ø NEXT P
```

Erase the Dot

Let's add a few new lines to the program to erase the dot:

```
4ØØ REM ** ERASE DOT
41Ø COLOR Ø
42Ø PLOT 1Ø,1Ø
```

The value of Ø in the COLOR command in line 41Ø tells the computer to plot a point the same color as the background screen. If we tell it to plot a dot with COLOR Ø in a place where another dot already exists, it will erase the dot that's there.

When you RUN this program, it puts the dot on the screen while it is playing the note, then erases the dot as the note stops playing.

RUN it again to make sure you really saw and heard what you thought you saw and heard!

Here's what ought to be happening:

While the note is playing:

When the note stops:

The word READY and the cursor appear in the text window when the program ends.

Now the complete listing should look like this:

```
1 REM *** SOUND AND COLOR
1Ø GRAPHICS 3
2Ø COLOR 1
3Ø PLOT 1Ø,1Ø

2ØØ REM ** VOICE Ø PLAYS MIDDLE C
21Ø SOUND Ø,121,1Ø,1Ø

3ØØ REM ** PAUSE–NOTE ON
31Ø FOR P=1 TO 5ØØ
32Ø NEXT P

4ØØ REM ** ERASE DOT
41Ø COLOR Ø
42Ø PLOT 1Ø,1Ø
```

INPUT STATEMENTS

What if you want to change the note this program plays without typing line 21Ø over again? You can do this by using an INPUT statement. Here's how it works.

First change line 21Ø to:

```
21Ø SOUND Ø,N,1Ø,1Ø
```

Now add an INPUT statement like this:

```
1ØØ REM ** CHOOSE YOUR NOTE
12Ø INPUT N
```

The INPUT statement must come *before* the SOUND statement where the N occurs here. We purposely skipped line 11Ø here because we're going to add a line there soon. You'll see!

Here's the listing now:

```
1 REM *** SOUND AND COLOR
10 GRAPHICS 3
20 COLOR 1
30 PLOT 10,10

100 REM ** CHOOSE YOUR NOTE
120 INPUT N

200 REM ** VOICE 0 PLAYS MIDDLE C
210 SOUND 0, N, 10,10

300 REM ** PAUSE—NOTE ON
310 FOR P=1 TO 500
320 NEXT P

400 REM ** ERASE DOT
410 COLOR 0
420 PLOT 10,10
```

Now when you RUN the program, here's what happens. You get this with no sound:

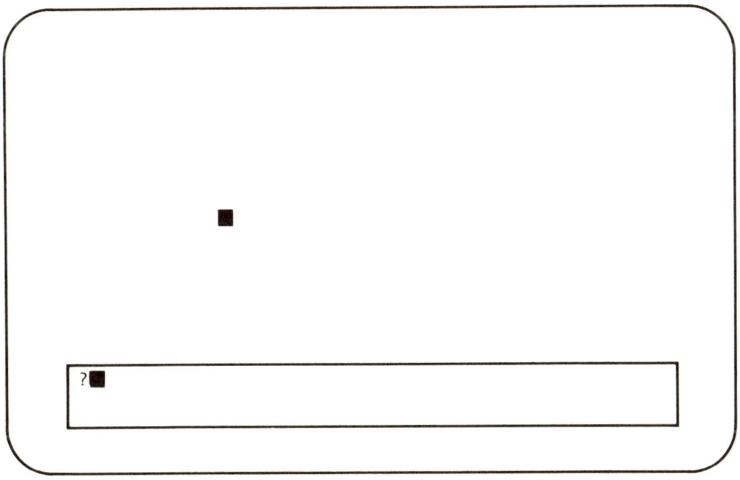

The machine is waiting for you to ENTER a note value.
Try typing 60 and press RETURN.
It plays the note!
You have to type RUN and press RETURN to start again.

Let's make some improvements.

First add a SOUND statement to turn off voice Ø after it plays:

```
500 REM ** VOICE 0 OFF
510 SOUND 0,0,0,0,
```

Now add:

```
800 GOTO 120
```

Now RUN it.

This time, when you ENTER a note value it plays the note and then prints another question mark.

To hear another note, just type another note value and press RETURN. You don't have to RUN the program again.

Here's the listing:

```
1 REM *** SOUND AND COLOR
10 GRAPHICS 3
20 COLOR 1
30 PLOT 10,10

100 REM ** CHOOSE YOUR NOTE
120 INPUT N

200 ** VOICE 0 PLAYS MIDDLE C
210 SOUND 0, N,10,10

300 REM ** PAUSE—NOTE ON
310 FOR P=1 TO 500
320 NEXT P

400 REM ** ERASE DOT
410 COLOR 0
420 PLOT 10,10

500 REM ** VOICE 0 OFF
510 SOUND 0,0,0,0
800 GOTO 120
```

Input Duration

You can use an INPUT statement for the length of the pause in line 31Ø like this:

Change line 31Ø to:

```
31Ø FOR P=1 TO Z
```

Then add:

```
15Ø REM ** DURATION
17Ø INPUT Z
```

What happens when you RUN it now?
First you get:

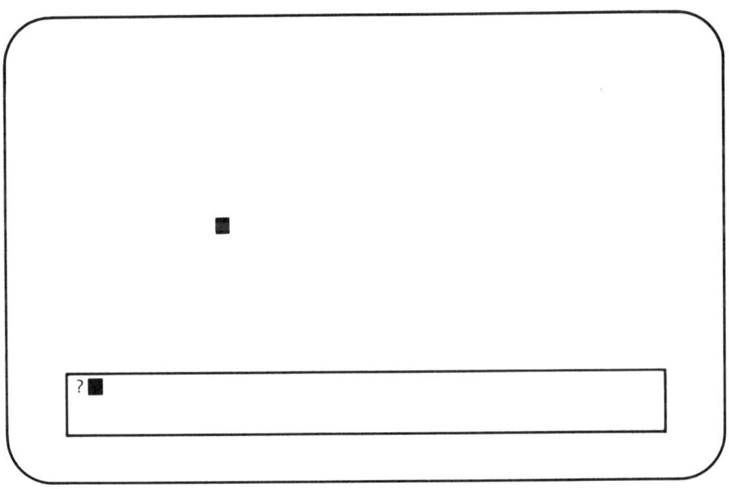

Then when you ENTER another note value, you get another question mark.

Type a number for duration and press RETURN. Now it plays the note!

The complete listing now looks like this:

```
1 REM *** SOUND AND COLOR
1Ø GRAPHICS 3
2Ø COLOR 1
3Ø PLOT 1Ø,1Ø

1ØØ REM ** CHOOSE YOUR NOTE
12Ø INPUT N

15Ø REM ** DURATION
17Ø INPUT Z

2ØØ REM ** VOICE Ø PLAYS MIDDLE C
21Ø SOUND Ø,N,1Ø,1Ø

3ØØ REM ** PAUSE–NOTE ON
31Ø FOR P=1 TO Z
32Ø NEXT P

4ØØ REM ** ERASE DOT
41Ø COLOR Ø
42Ø PLOT 1Ø,1Ø

5ØØ REM ** VOICE Ø OFF
51Ø SOUND Ø,Ø,Ø,Ø
8ØØ GOTO 12Ø
```

PRINT STATEMENTS

The computer can print instructions in the text window to make things clearer. To do this, use a PRINT statement.
For example, add:

```
11Ø PRINT "CHOOSE YOUR NOTE"
```

and:

```
16Ø PRINT "HOW LONG DOES IT PLAY"
17Ø INPUT Z
```

Finally, change line 8ØØ to:

```
8ØØ GOTO 11Ø
```

Now when you RUN it you get:

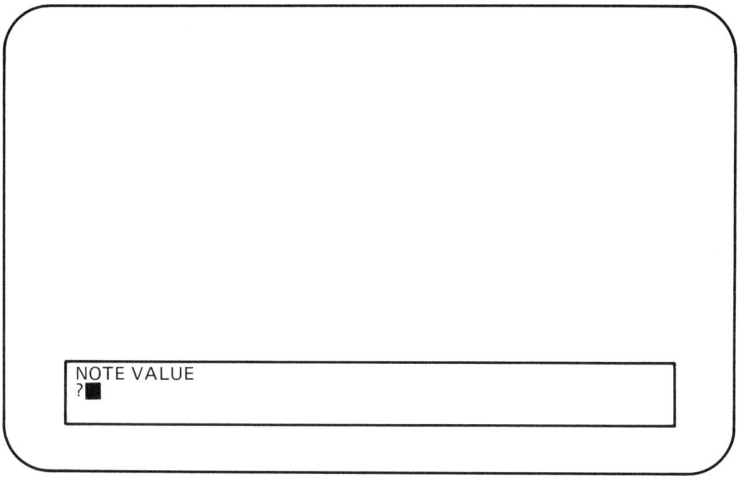

And then:

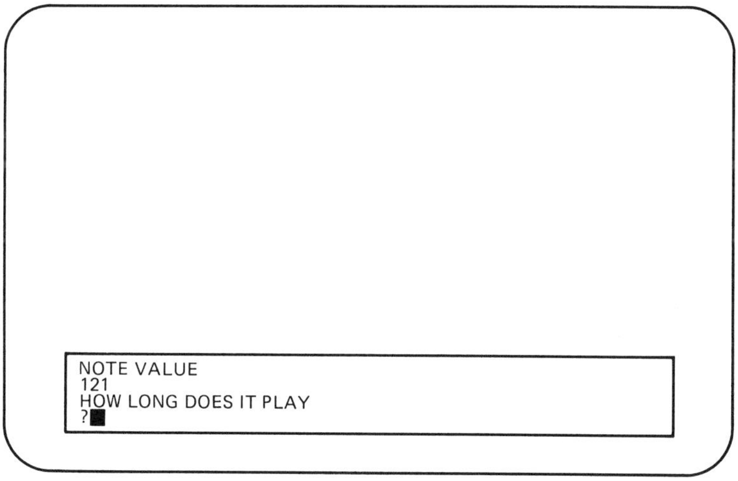

Then it plays your note and asks for another one, and so on.

Here's the complete listing now.

```
1 REM *** SOUND AND COLOR
10 GRAPHICS 3
20 COLOR 1
30 PLOT 10,10

100 REM ** CHOOSE YOUR NOTE
120 INPUT N
150 REM ** DURATION
160 PRINT "HOW LONG DOES IT PLAY"
170 INPUT Z

200 REM ** VOICE 0 PLAYS MIDDLE C
210 SOUND 0,N,10,10

300 REM ** PAUSE—NOTE ON
310 FOR P=1 TO Z
320 NEXT P

400 REM ** ERASE DOT
410 COLOR 0
420 PLOT 10,10

500 REM ** VOICE 0 OFF
510 SOUND 0,0,0,0
800 GOTO 120
```

Before you start the exercises, you might like to know about another convenient point of grammar in ATARI BASIC.

Multiple-Line Statements

ATARI BASIC allows you to combine two or more commands on one line of a program. To do this, you must separate the commands with a colon (:).

For example, a COLOR command and a graphics mode 3 command might be combined as follows:

```
110 GRAPHICS 3: COLOR 2
```

instead of:

```
110 GRAPHICS 3
120 COLOR 2
```

Some programmers use multiple-line statements to put a REM statement on the same line as the command it describes.

```
12Ø INPUT N:REM ** CHOOSE YOUR NOTE
```

You actually won't see too many uses of multiple-line statements in this book because we want to list the programs in a way that is easy for you to read. We wanted you to know about this concept though, so you can use it if you wish.

READ AND DATA STATEMENTS

To play an entire melody, you can enter a SOUND statement for each note, but there are easier ways to do it.

One way is to use READ and DATA statements together. This allows you to ENTER several note values as DATA and have the computer READ them into the SOUND statement.

Type NEW and press RETURN to clear the last program from the computer's memory. Now ENTER this program which plays ten notes:

```
1 REM ** YOUR OWN SONG

1ØØ REM ** READS THE NOTE
11Ø READ N

2ØØ REM ** PLAYS NOTE
21Ø SOUND Ø,N,1Ø,1Ø

3ØØ REM PAUSE
31Ø FOR P=1 TO 1ØØ
32Ø NEXT P

4ØØ REM ** NEXT NOTE
41Ø GOTO 11Ø

5ØØ REM ** THE NOTE VALUES
51Ø DATA 121,81,96,6Ø,64
52Ø DATA 35,45,64,1Ø8,121
```

This line

READS

This Data

RUN it and you'll hear your ATARI Computer play a melody. When it gets finished, you'll get an ERROR message:

```
ERROR-     6 AT LINE 11Ø
```

This doesn't mean there is anything wrong; it just means the computer can't find any more DATA to READ.

Here's how this program works. In lines 51Ø and 52Ø you've entered note values from the chart on page 9 as DATA.

When the program RUNs, the READ statement in line 11Ø tells the computer to READ the first note value from the DATA statement. That value is 121. It plays that note in line 21Ø.

When it gets to line 41Ø, the machine goes back to line 11Ø, and this time it READs the second value for N (which is 81) in the DATA statement and then plays it. It does this until it has read all the DATA.

We've used just ten notes here, but you can use as many as you want. You can put more than five numbers per line in a DATA statement, but it's easier to see what you're doing if you put only a few numbers on each line.

How about some dots with this one? Just add lines:

```
25Ø REM ** PLOT SOME POINTS
26Ø GR. 5
27Ø COLOR 2
28Ø PLOT N/2,25
```

Graphics mode 5 has 8Ø columns and 8Ø rows. Since none of the values for N in the DATA statement are more than 16Ø, we can divide N by 2 and use that value for the column in a PLOT statement (line 28Ø), if we use graphics mode 5. All of the dots will be plotted in row 1Ø

In this program, the machine enters the graphics mode each time it goes through the loop. When it does this, it erases what it had plotted on the screen before. That's why each dot disappears before the next one appears.

Now the complete listing is:

```
1 REM ** "YOUR OWN SONG

100 REM ** READS THE NOTE
110 READ N

200 REM ** PLAYS THE NOTE
210 SOUND 0,N,10,10
250 REM ** PLOT SOME POINTS
260 GRAPHICS 5
270 COLOR 2
280 PLOT N/2,10

300 REM ** PAUSE
310 FOR P=1 TO 100
320 NEXT P

400 REM ** NEXT NOTE
410 GOTO 110

500 REM ** THE NOTE VALUES
510 DATA 121,81,96,60,64
520 DATA 35,45,64,108,121
```

Well, by now you're ready to play some tunes of your own, so go to it! Keep the program for the Self-Test that follows.

Self-Test

1. What do you need in line 310 to make the note stay on?

```
210 SOUND 0,121,10,10
300 REM ** SOUND STAYS ON
310_______________
```

2. How do you make the computer count to itself in ATARI BASIC?
3. Will this be a fast or a slow note?

```
110 SOUND 0,121,10,10
210 FOR P=1 TO 10
220 NEXT P
```

4. What value for COLOR do you use in line 410 to erase the dot?

5. What statement is used to enter information while a program is running?
6. Why won't this program work to INPUT notes?

```
1ØØ REM ** CHOOSE YOUR NOTE
11Ø INPUT N
```

7. Can you INPUT more than one variable in a program?
8. If you wanted to enter several tone values in the computer's memory and then use them one by one in a SOUND statement, what two statements would work together to do this?

Answers

1. `31Ø GOTO 21Ø` or `31Ø GOTO 31Ø`
2. With a FOR-NEXT loop
3. Fast
4. COLOR Ø
5. An INPUT statement
6. The SOUND statement in line 21Ø needs to be:

```
2ØØ SOUND Ø,N,1Ø,1Ø
```

7. Yes, but you need an INPUT statement for each variable. For example:

```
11Ø INPUT N
12Ø INPUT T
21Ø SOUND Ø,N,T,Ø
```

8. READ and DATA

Challenges

1. Write a program that lets you INPUT tone as a variable in the SOUND statement.
2. Write a program using READ and DATA to plot some points.

CHAPTER FIVE

Some Special Effects with Sound

In the last chapter we used a FOR-NEXT loop to tell the computer to count to itself for a moment when we wanted it to pause.

The FOR-NEXT loop can also be used in other ways. In this chapter we'll begin to explore some ways to use the FOR-NEXT loop to have the computer ENTER values for different notes in the SOUND statement.

ENTER NOTES WITH A FOR-NEXT LOOP

Suppose you want to ENTER every value for note Ø to 255 in a SOUND statement. Instead of doing a lot of typing, you can get the machine to ENTER each value for you by using a FOR-NEXT loop like this:

Optional (lines 1, 1ØØ and 2ØØ)

```
1 REM *** DESCENDING PITCH

1ØØ REM ** BEGINS LOOP
11Ø FOR N=Ø TO 255
12Ø SOUND Ø,N,1Ø,1Ø

2ØØ REM ** ASSIGNS NEXT NOTE VALUE
21Ø NEXT N
```

ENTER and RUN this program to hear what is sounds like. You should hear a rapidly descending pitch.

As the loop begins, N is assigned a value of Ø in line 11Ø. This value is then used in the SOUND statement in line 12Ø. The next time through the cycle, N is given a value of 1, and the next time N is given a value of 2, and so on until all 256 notes have been played.

You may recall from Chapter 1 that the lower the number value for the note variable, the higher the note. That is, a note value of Ø is very high, while 256 is very low. That's why the note descends in pitch.

We will use REM statements as we introduce new lines to programs from here on, but you don't need to include them in order for the programs to RUN properly.

Want to hear it repeat? Just add:

```
3ØØ REM ** STARTS AGAIN
31Ø GOTO 11Ø
```

Your listing will now look like this:

```
1 REM *** DESCENDING PITCH

1ØØ REM ** BEGINS LOOP
11Ø FOR N=Ø TO 255
12Ø SOUND Ø,N,1Ø,1Ø

2ØØ REM ** ASSIGNS NEXT NOTE VALUE
21Ø NEXT N

3ØØ REM ** STARTS AGAIN
31Ø GOTO 11Ø
```

Now when you RUN the program you hear it play the cycle just as it did before, but when it gets to line 31Ø it will go back to line 11Ø and start the cycle again. This continues until you press the SYSTEM RESET key to get out of the program. Give it a try to hear it for yourself.

USE THE BREAK KEY AND THEN CONTINUE

There's another way to get out of a program and then back into it that will produce an interesting result with this particular program.

First RUN the program and leave it going.

Now press the BREAK key at the upper right corner of the keyboard. What happens?

You'll get a message like this on the screen:

```
STOPPED AT LINE 12Ø
```

Meanwhile, the sound stays on, but the pitch stops falling and remains constant at some single note (it might be high; it might be low).

Now type CONT and press RETURN.

What happens this time?

It goes back to a falling tone, picking up the cycle from wherever it was when you pressed the BREAK key. Leave the cycle going for a while again.

Now press the BREAK key again.

You'll most probably get a different note when it stops this time. This is because when you press the BREAK key, although the machine stops running the program, it leaves the voice on with whatever note value has just been entered in the SOUND statement. So wherever you are in the FOR-NEXT loop when you press BREAK, that's the note you'll get.

A little more experimentation with this idea will give you a good sense of how the FOR-NEXT loop is working in this program.

RUN the program.
Press BREAK.
Type CONT and press RETURN.
Press BREAK.
Type CONT and press RETURN.
And so on. . . .

PAUSE WITHIN THE CYCLE

If you want to slow down the rate at which the cycle occurs and thus stretch the sound out, you can use the FOR-NEXT loop to pause the way you learned in the last chapter. For example, add the following lines to the program:

```
150 REM ** PAUSE
160 FOR P=1 TO 100
170 NEXT P
```

The complete listing should now be:

```
1 REM *** DESCENDING PITCH

100 REM ** BEGINS LOOP
110 FOR N=0 TO 255
120 SOUND 0,N,10,10

150 REM ** PAUSE
160 FOR P=1 TO 100
170 NEXT P

200 REM ** ASSIGNS NEXT NOTE VALUE
210 NEXT N

300 REM ** STARTS AGAIN
310 GOTO 110
```

Slows down rate at which the pitch falls (lines 160–170)

RUN the program this way to hear what it sounds like.

The pause loop here is an example of a *nested FOR-NEXT* loop; that is, one FOR-NEXT loop that occurs within another. The nested loop must be completely within the other loop. For example, the pause loop here must be placed after line 110, but before line 210.

This will not work:

Improper nesting of loops

```
1 REM *** DESCENDING PITCH

1ØØ REM ** BEGINS LOOP
11Ø FOR N=Ø TO 255
12Ø SOUND Ø,N,1Ø,1Ø

15Ø REM ** PAUSE
16Ø FOR P=1 TO 1ØØ
165 NEXT N
17Ø NEXT P

2ØØ REM ** ASSIGNS NEXT NOTE VALUE
31Ø GOTO 11Ø
```

Make sure you have this listing before going on to the next section:

Properly nested loops–one within the other

note loop

pause loop

```
1 REM *** DESCENDING PITCH
1ØØ REM ** BEGINS LOOP
11Ø FOR N=Ø TO 255
12Ø SOUND Ø,N,1Ø,1Ø

15Ø REM ** PAUSE
16Ø FOR P=1 TO 1ØØ
17Ø NEXT P

2ØØ REM ** ASSIGNS NEXT NOTE VALUE
21Ø NEXT N

3ØØ REM ** STARTS AGAIN
31Ø GOTO 11Ø
```

Vary the Length of the Pause

If you change the length of the pause in line 16Ø, it will create some different effects. To explore this, you can use an INPUT statement that you also learned in Chapter 4. Here's an example of how that might be done:

```
1 REM *** DESCENDING PITCH
4Ø PRINT "LENGTH OF PAUSE"
5Ø INPUT X

1ØØ REM ** BEGINS LOOP
11Ø FOR N=Ø TO 255
12Ø SOUND Ø,N,1Ø,1Ø

15Ø REM ** PAUSE
16Ø FOR P=1 TO X
17Ø NEXT P

2ØØ REM ** ASSIGNS NEXT NOTE VALUE
21Ø NEXT N

3ØØ REM ** STARTS AGAIN
31Ø GOTO 11Ø
```

These lines allow you to choose length of pause (arrows point to lines 5Ø and 16Ø)

Once you've made the changes described here, experiment a bit with different lengths for the pause before going on to the next section. But keep the program for the next section.

DELETE LINES FROM THE PROGRAM

Often you will wish to remove or delete lines from a program. The way to do this with ATARI BASIC is to simply type the line number of the line you wish to delete and then press RETURN.

Suppose, for example, you wanted to remove the REM statement from the following program:

```
1ØØ REM ** MAKES A NOTE
11Ø SOUND Ø,121,1Ø,1Ø
```

You can remove line 1ØØ by simply typing:

```
1ØØ
```

And pressing RETURN.

If you still have the program with which we've been working, let's practice this technique a little.

First, LIST your program to see if this is what you have:

```
1 REM *** DESCENDING PITCH
4Ø PRINT "LENGTH OF PAUSE"
5Ø INPUT X

1ØØ REM ** BEGINS LOOP
11Ø FOR N=Ø TO 255
12Ø SOUND Ø,N,1Ø,1Ø

15Ø REM ** PAUSE
16Ø FOR P=1 TO X
17Ø NEXT P

2ØØ REM ** ASSIGNS NEXT NOTE VALUE
21Ø NEXT N

3ØØ REM ** STARTS AGAIN
31Ø GOTO 11Ø
```

If you have something slightly different it's okay because we're going to delete several lines anyway. Let's delete some lines as follows:

* Type 4Ø (and press RETURN).

* Type 5Ø (and press RETURN).

* Type 15Ø (and press RETURN).

* Type 16Ø (and press RETURN).

* Type 17Ø (and press RETURN).

You've just removed the PRINT statement, the INPUT statement, and the pause loop. The program should now look like this:

```
1 REM *** DESCENDING PITCH

1ØØ REM ** BEGINS LOOP
11Ø FOR N=Ø TO 255
12Ø SOUND Ø,N,1Ø,1Ø

2ØØ REM ** ASSIGNS NEXT NOTE VALUE
21Ø NEXT N

3ØØ REM ** STARTS AGAIN
31Ø GOTO 11Ø
```

If you have something different, make whatever changes are necessary to come up with this listing. You can delete lines as described and also use the editing features you learned in Chapter 1 to move the cursor with the CTRL key and the arrow keys on the upper right corner of the keyboard.

If it seems easier to just type NEW and ENTER the program from scratch, that's fine too. But make sure you have the same listing as above because we'll use it in the next section.

PLAY A PORTION OF THE NOTE SPECTRUM

You can create a number of different sounds by playing only a portion of the note spectrum. For example, to play only note values Ø through 1Ø inclusive, change line 11Ø of your program to:

```
11Ø FOR N=Ø TO 1Ø
```

This is the high end of the spectrum, and also a short cycle, so it produces a rapidly repeating, high-pitched sound, sort of like a bird chirping. The complete listing should now look like this:

```
1 REM *** DESCENDING PITCH

1ØØ REM ** BEGINS LOOP
11Ø FOR N=Ø TO 1Ø          <- Plays a portion of the note spectrum
12Ø SOUND Ø,N,1Ø,1Ø

2ØØ REM ** ASSIGNS NEXT NOTE VALUE
21Ø NEXT N

3ØØ REM ** STARTS AGAIN
31Ø GOTO 11Ø
```

ENTER and RUN the program so you'll hear it for yourself.

Before you look at the next program, see if you can think of a way to use an INPUT statement to vary the length of the sequence.

Here's what we came up with.

Vary length of note sequence

```
1 REM *** DESCENDING PITCH

4Ø PRINT "LENGTH OF PAUSE"
5Ø INPUT Z

1ØØ REM ** BEGINS LOOP
11Ø FOR N=Ø TO Z
12Ø SOUND Ø,N,1Ø,1Ø

2ØØ REM ** ASSIGNS NEXT NOTE VALUE
21Ø NEXT N

3ØØ REM ** STARTS AGAIN
31Ø GOTO 11Ø
```

Play a Portion from the Middle of the Spectrum

You don't have to start counting with Ø in a FOR-NEXT loop, so it's possible to play a sequence of notes from somewhere within the spectrum of notes. For example, to play a sequence with note values from 1ØØ to 15Ø, change line 11Ø to:

```
11Ø FOR N=1ØØ TO 15Ø
```

and then RUN the program.

To further explore this concept, you can INPUT a variable at either end of the sequence something like this:

Vary both ends of note sequence

```
1 REM *** DESCENDING PITCH
2Ø PRINT "BEGINNING OF LOOP"
3Ø INPUT A
5Ø INPUT Z

1ØØ REM ** BEGINS LOOP
11Ø FOR N=A TO Z
12Ø SOUND Ø,N,1Ø,1Ø

2ØØ REM ** ASSIGNS NEXT NOTE VALUE
21Ø NEXT N

3ØØ REM ** STARTS AGAIN
31Ø GOTO 11Ø
```

We encourage you to ENTER these programs (don't forget your editing tools) and then give these concepts a thorough exploration before going on. This will give you many ideas to use in later programs.

COUNTING BY STEPS

Just as you might run up stairs skipping two or three steps at a time, the computer can count in multiples of 2, 5, 1Ø, or whatever. To do this, use the STEP function with the FOR-NEXT loop, as in line 11Ø of the program below.

Rather than acting as a separate command, the STEP function becomes a part of the FOR statement.

```
1 REM *** DESCENDING PITCH

1ØØ REM ** BEGINS LOOP
11Ø FOR N=Ø TO 255 STEP 1Ø    <-- STEP function to count by 10s
12Ø SOUND Ø,N,1Ø,1Ø

2ØØ REM ** ASSIGNS NEXT NOTE VALUE
21Ø NEXT N

3ØØ REM ** STARTS AGAIN
31Ø GOTO 11Ø
```

ENTER and RUN this program to hear what it sounds like. Values of Ø, 1Ø, 2Ø, and so on are now being entered for note in the SOUND statement in line 12Ø. Consequently, only twenty-five notes are played each time through the sequence. This makes the loop shorter and, as you can hear, makes a sound that your ears can hear better than our words can describe.

If you want to count by 5's, just change line 11Ø to:

```
11Ø FOR N=Ø TO 255 STEP 5
```

Now make the STEP function a variable and use an INPUT statement to explore counting at different intervals.

Here's how we did it:

These lines are added → (lines 40 and 50)

STEP as a variable → (line 110)

```
1 REM *** DESCENDING PITCH
40 PRINT "ENTER A VALUE FOR STEP"
50 INPUT S

100 REM ** BEGINS LOOP
110 FOR N=0 TO 255 STEP S
120 SOUND 0,N,10,10

200 REM ** ASSIGNS NEXT NOTE VALUE
210 NEXT N

300 REM ** STARTS AGAIN
310 GOTO 110
```

Counting Backwards

You can also have the computer count backwards. For example, here's a program to play a sequence starting with the lowest note (N = 255) and going to the highest (N = 0):

Counts backwards → (line 110)

```
1 REM *** ASCENDING PITCH

100 REM ** BEGINS LOOP
110 FOR N=255 TO 0 STEP -1
120 SOUND 0,N,10,10

200 REM ** ASSIGNS NEXT NOTE VALUE
210 NEXT N

300 REM ** STARTS AGAIN
310 GOTO 110
```

ENTER and RUN this program to hear the note spectrum played in reverse. Save yourself some typing by editing out lines 40 and 50 of the previous program and then changing line 110.

You can also play different portions of the spectrum in reverse just as you did going from high pitch to low pitch. For example:

```
1 REM *** ASCENDING PITCH

1ØØ REM ** BEGINS LOOP
11Ø FOR N=15Ø TO 5Ø STEP -1
12Ø SOUND Ø,N,1Ø,1Ø

2ØØ REM ** ASSIGNS NEXT NOTE VALUE
21Ø NEXT N

3ØØ REM ** STARTS AGAIN
31Ø GOTO 11Ø
```

You can also count backwards by intervals. For example:

Count backwards by STEPS → line 11Ø

```
1 REM *** ASCENDING PITCH

1ØØ REM ** BEGINS LOOP
11Ø FOR N=255 TO Ø STEP -25
12Ø SOUND Ø,N,1Ø,1Ø

2ØØ REM ** ASSIGNS NEXT NOTE VALUE
21Ø NEXT N

3ØØ REM ** STARTS AGAIN
31Ø GOTO 11Ø
```

ENTER and RUN this program to hear what it sounds like.

The parameters in the FOR statement in line 11Ø can be made variables and explored with an INPUT statement just as you did when counting forwards. For example, make the STEP function a variable counting backwards like this:

Vary STEP counting backwards → lines 5Ø and 11Ø

```
1 REM *** ASCENDING PITCH
4Ø PRINT "ENTER A VALUE FOR STEP"
5Ø INPUT S

1ØØ REM ** BEGINS LOOP
11Ø FOR N=255 TO Ø STEP -S
12Ø SOUND Ø,N,1Ø,1Ø

2ØØ REM ** ASSIGNS NEXT NOTE VALUE
21Ø NEXT N

3ØØ REM ** STARTS AGAIN
31Ø GOTO 11Ø
```

ENTER and RUN this program to experiment with how counting backwards at different intervals affects the sound.

Now see if you can change the program to use an INPUT statement to play part of the note spectrum backwards. We'll give one example; you try a few others.

INPUT portion of note spectrum backwards (lines 5Ø and 11Ø)

```
1 REM *** ASCENDING PITCH
4Ø PRINT "END OF LOOP"
45 PRINT "MUST BE LESS THAN 1ØØ"
5Ø INPUT Z

1ØØ REM ** BEGINS LOOP
11Ø FOR N=1ØØ TO Z STEP -1
12Ø SOUND Ø,N,1Ø,1Ø

2ØØ REM ** ASSIGNS NEXT NOTE VALUE
21Ø NEXT N

3ØØ REM ** STARTS AGAIN
31Ø GOTO 11Ø
```

Pause While Counting Backwards

Again, you can slow down the sequence of notes played backwards by adding a FOR-NEXT loop to pause like this:

Add these lines to pause (lines 16Ø and 17Ø)

```
1 REM *** ASCENDING PITCH

1ØØ REM ** BEGINS LOOP
11Ø FOR N=1ØØ TO Z STEP -1
12Ø SOUND Ø,N,1Ø,1Ø

15Ø REM ** PAUSE
16Ø FOR P=1 TO 1ØØ
17Ø NEXT P

2ØØ REM ** ASSIGNS NEXT NOTE VALUE
21Ø NEXT N

3ØØ REM ** STARTS AGAIN
31Ø GOTO 11Ø
```

Remember, this is a nested loop, so be sure it is entirely within the loop for note sequence. Now add an INPUT statement to the program and vary the length of the pause in the program.

Back-to-Back Loops

You can get some interesting effects by having a loop with falling pitch followed by a loop with rising pitch, like this:

```
1 REM ** BIRD SOUND

100 REM ** FALLING PITCH
110 FOR N=0 TO 100
120 SOUND 0,N,10,10
190 NEXT N

200 REM ** RISING PITCH
210 FOR N=100 TO 0 STEP -1
220 SOUND 0,N,10,10
290 NEXT N

300 REM ** STARTS AGAIN
310 GOTO 110
```

When you ENTER and RUN this program, you'll get another kind of bird sound than when you used a loop going in only one direction.

For an experiment, try making the first loop play a longer cycle of notes, like this:

```
100 REM ** FALLING PITCH
110 FOR N=0 TO 50
```

while the second loop plays a short cycle:

```
100 REM ** RISING PITCH
110 FOR N=10 TO 0 STEP -1
```

ENTER these lines and RUN the program to hear the latest sound. Of course, you can do it the other way around. That is, make the first loop short and the second loop long.

There's room to add a FOR-NEXT to pause between lines 120 and 190 or between 220 and 290, so be sure to experiment with the effects created by doing that.

A BRIEF REVIEW

So far in this chapter you've learned to use a FOR-NEXT loop to:

- Play all or part of the note spectrum.
- Count backwards through the note range.
- Count by steps both backwards and forwards.
- Create a rising and falling pitch by using back-to-back loops.

You have also learned to use a nested loop to pause after each note.

We suggest that you thoroughly explore these possibilities before going on. You'll undoubtedly discover many things we haven't thought to mention.

Try to write programs using INPUT statements to explore some different parameters. For example, try to INPUT different values for tone (even numbers 0 to 14). Remember, tone is the third parameter in the SOUND statement.

As you do this, you'll probably get some ERROR messages. Don't be discouraged. Every programmer, no matter how skilled, experiences this. Sometimes you find out what the rules of a particular language (in this case ATARI BASIC) are by just trying things to see if they work.

As a matter of fact, we didn't just sit down and type in the programs you see in this book. We got several ERROR messages before we got them the way we wanted them.

There's an ancient Chinese proverb that goes something like:

```
* * * * * * * * * * * * * * * * * * * * * * * *
 RIGHTEOUS PERSISTENCE BRINGS GOOD FORTUNE
* * * * * * * * * * * * * * * * * * * * * * * *
```

PITCH GOES BOTH WAYS

Another way to have the computer count is shown in lines 110 and 120 of the following program:

```
100 REM ** SUBTRACTION METHOD
110 FOR N=0 TO 255

210 SOUND 0,255-N,10,10

310 NEXT N

410 GOTO 110
```

ENTER and RUN this program and you'll hear the pitch of the sound rising just as it would if lines 11Ø and 21Ø were:

```
11Ø FOR N=255 TO Ø STEP -1
21Ø SOUND Ø,N,1Ø,1Ø
```

In the version we've used above, where the computer subtracts the value of N from 255 in the SOUND statement each time through the loop, here's what happens.

First, line 11Ø gives N a value of Ø. Then, in the SOUND statement in line 21Ø the note value becomes:

255 – Ø = 255

Next time through the cycle, N gets a value of 1. So the note value in the SOUND statement becomes:

255 – 1 = 254

And so on through the entire loop.

This method of counting through the loop backwards gives you the opportunity to have the pitch of two voices going in opposite directions within one FOR-NEXT loop. You use two SOUND statements to do this, as follows:

```
1ØØ REM ** PITCH GOES BOTH WAYS
11Ø FOR N=Ø TO 255

21Ø SOUND Ø,N,1Ø,1Ø
26Ø SOUND 1,255-N,1Ø,1Ø

31Ø NEXT N

41Ø GOTO 11Ø
```

ENTER and RUN this program to hear the sound it creates. Line 21Ø is playing note values beginning at Ø and increasing to 255, thus causing a rising pitch. Line 26Ø is playing notes going in the opposite direction; that is from 255 to Ø, thus creating a falling pitch. Figure 5–1 pictures what's happening.

You can use this technique to have a rising and falling pitch converge upon some note in the middle of the spectrum. That is, they stop rising or falling when they get to the same note and continue to play that note.

Figure 5–1 Two Voices Going in Opposite Directions

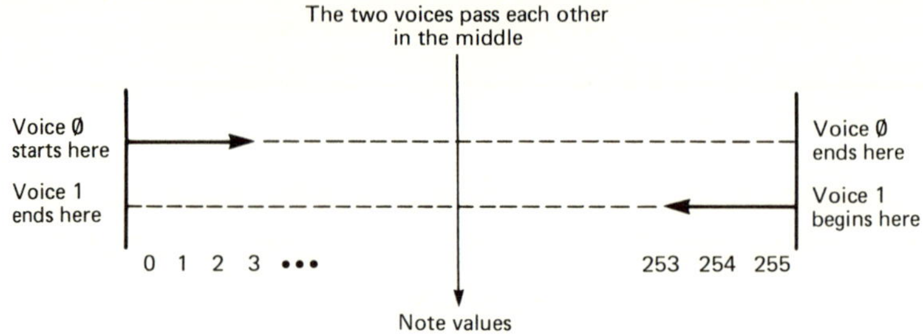

ENTER and RUN this program to hear a rising and falling pitch converge upon a single note:

```
1ØØ REM ** CONVERGING TO SINGLE NOTE
11Ø FOR N=Ø TO 125

21Ø SOUND Ø,N,1Ø,1Ø
26Ø SOUND 1,25Ø-N,1Ø,1Ø

31Ø NEXT N

41Ø GOTO 41Ø
```

Figure 5–2 pictures this phenomenon.

Figure 5–2 Two Voices Converge and Play a Single Sustained Note

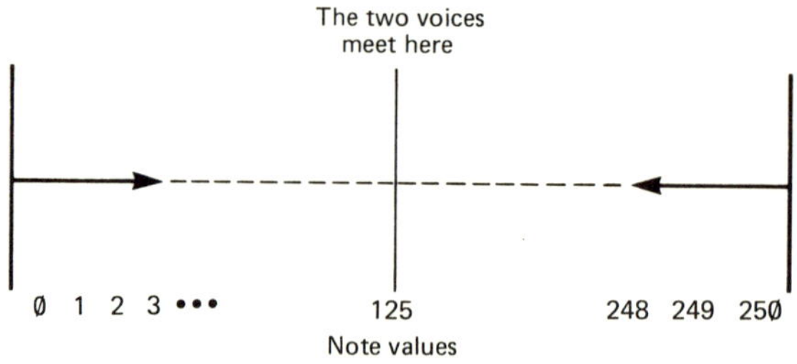

You can use this technique playing part of the spectrum as well. You might have something like this:

```
100 REM ** PITCH GOES BOTH WAYS
110 FOR N=40 TO 50

210 SOUND 0,N,10,10
260 SOUND 1,100-N,10,10

310 NEXT N

410 GOTO 410
```

Plays note values from 60 to 50 (→ line 260)

ENTER and RUN this program and then try some variations on lines 110 and 260 for yourself.

PAUSE BETWEEN THE VOICES

A short loop to pause between the two voices will give you yet another sound, but it will be most effective if you turn off each voice (as you learned in Chapter 4) while the other voice is playing. The following program gives an example of how this might be done:

```
100 REM ** SUBTRACTION METHOD
110 FOR N=0 TO 250

200 REM ** HIGH NOTES
210 SOUND 0,250-N,10,10
220 FOR P=1 TO 5
230 NEXT P
240 SOUND 0,0,0,0

250 REM ** LOW NOTES
260 SOUND 0,250-N,10,10
270 FOR P=1 TO 5
280 NEXT P
290 SOUND 1,0,0,0

310 NEXT N

410 GOTO 410
```

Causes note for each voice to be played separately (→ lines 240 and 290)

As you may have guessed, there is plenty of room to explore here, by changing the length of one or both of the pause loops in this program. Once again, the INPUT statement can help you explore these possibilities. Also try using different values for the tone parameter in the SOUND statement with this program. Remember, tone is even numbers from Ø to 14 inclusive.

We'll look at some ways to use three and four voices to create sound effects later, but don't be afraid to try programs using three or four voices on your own now. You'll probably find plenty of things we haven't thought of.

ATTACK AND DECAY

Have you ever wondered what makes a piano playing the note middle C sound different from a violin playing the same note?

Actually many factors contribute to the characteristic sound of a particular instrument. As a matter of fact, a very exciting science called *psychoacoustics* studies these factors in detail. We won't be able to go very deeply into the nature of sound in this book, but we will look at a few ways to "shape" notes with ATARI BASIC.

Two very important factors contributing to the shape of a note are its attack and its decay.

Attack

The attack of a note refers to how fast it reaches its maximum volume. A note with a fast attack (typical of the piano) will reach its maximum volume very quickly. A note with a slow attack (typical of the violin) will take longer to reach its maximum volume. This is pictured in Figure 5–3.

You can affect the attack of a note with ATARI BASIC by using a FOR-NEXT loop with the loudness parameter of the SOUND statement. To explore this, first ENTER and RUN the following program:

```
12Ø SOUND Ø,121,1Ø,1Ø
31Ø FOR P=Ø TO 5ØØ
32Ø NEXT P
```

It briefly plays the note middle C as you would expect. Now RUN the

Figure 5–3 Slow Attack–Fast Decay

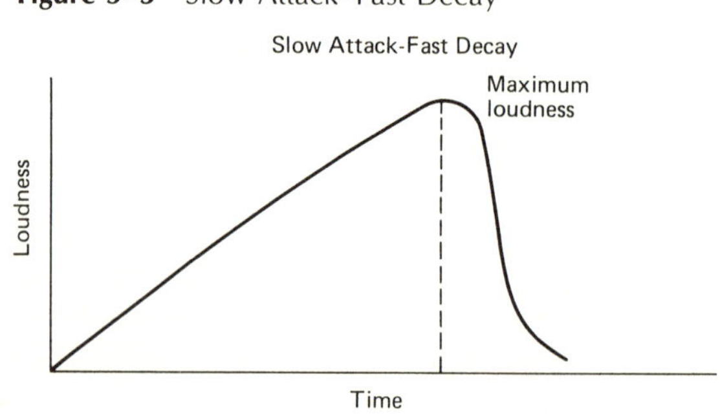

program a few more times, paying very close attention to how the sound starts. If you type RUN and then wait a few seconds before you press RETURN, it will help you with this experiment.

Once you've done that, add the following lines to the program:

```
1ØØ REM ** ATTACK LOOP
11Ø FOR L=Ø TO 15
19Ø NEXT L
```

Also change line 12Ø to:

```
12Ø SOUND Ø,121,1Ø,L
```

Your program listing should now look like this:

Changes attack of note (→ lines 11Ø and 19Ø)

```
1ØØ REM ** ATTACK LOOP
11Ø FOR L=Ø TO 15
12Ø SOUND Ø,121,1Ø,L
19Ø NEXT L
299 REM
31Ø FOR P=Ø TO 5ØØ
32Ø NEXT P
```

When you ENTER and RUN this program, you'll hear that the note doesn't have such an abrupt beginning as it did before. This is because the attack is much slower.

You can slow the attack of the note in this program even further by adding a very short pause loop as follows:

```
15Ø REM ** PAUSE
16Ø FOR P=1 TO 1Ø
17Ø NEXT P
```

The program listing now looks like this:

Slower attack (→ lines 16Ø and 17Ø)

```
1ØØ REM ** ATTACK LOOP
11Ø FOR L=Ø TO 15
12Ø SOUND Ø,121,1Ø,L

15Ø REM ** PAUSE
16Ø FOR P=1 TO 1Ø
17Ø NEXT P

19Ø NEXT L
299 REM
31Ø FOR P=Ø TO 1ØØ
32Ø NEXT P
```

Changes in the length of the pause in lines 160 and 170 will produce variations in the attack of the note. It is worth exploring. See if you can make some changes in the program to do this with an INPUT statement; then have a look at our program below.

Program to INPUT changes in attack of note:

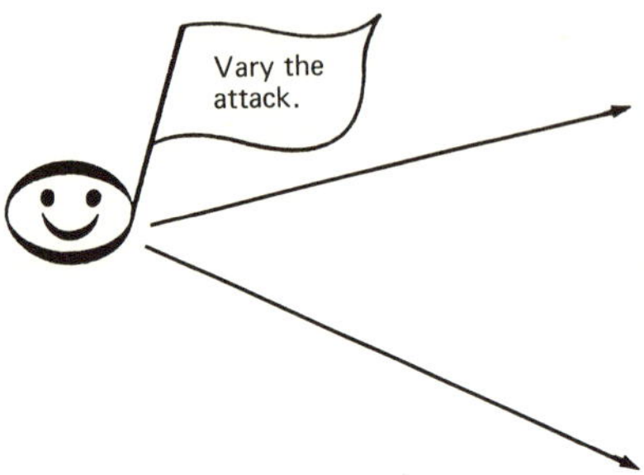


```
20 PRINT "THE HIGHER THE NUMBER"
30 PRINT "THE SLOWER THE ATTACK"
40 PRINT "WHAT VALUE FOR ATTACK"

50 INPUT A

100 REM ** ATTACK LOOP
110 FOR L=0 TO 15
120 SOUND 0,121,10,L

150 REM ** PAUSE
160 FOR P=1 TO A
170 NEXT P
190 NEXT L

200 REM ** PLAYS NOTE A WHILE
210 FOR P=1 TO 100
220 NEXT P
```

Decay

The speed with which the loudness of a note falls off after reaching its maximum loudness is called the *decay* of the note.

To affect the decay of a note, use the FOR-NEXT loop to count the loudness parameter in reverse. For example:

```
300 REM ** DECAY LOOP
310 FOR L=15 TO 0 STEP -1
320 SOUND 0,121,10,L

390 NEXT L
```

ENTER and RUN this short program. It plays the note pretty fast, but there is a slight decay on the note. Run it a few more times, and then add this nested loop to pause within the decay loop.

```
350 REM ** PAUSE
360 FOR P=1 TO 10
370 NEXT P
```

Now your complete listing should look like this:

```
3ØØ REM ** DECAY LOOP
31Ø FOR L=15 TO Ø STEP -1
32Ø SOUND Ø,121,1Ø,L

35Ø REM ** PAUSE
36Ø FOR P=1 TO 1Ø
37Ø NEXT P

39Ø NEXT L
```

This begins to give the note a shape closer to that of a harpsichord. Notice that in this case we are not using a loop to slow down the attack of the note, so it has a fast attack and a slow decay. This is pictured in Figure 5–4.

It may seem like you are doing a lot of programming just to make such minor changes in the sound of a single note, but you'll soon learn how to use these loops with a READ–DATA program similar to the one you used in Chapter 4. While you still have the decay loop though, see if you can change the pause loop and use an INPUT statement to affect the decay. Then have a look at how we did it below.

Program to INPUT decay as a variable:

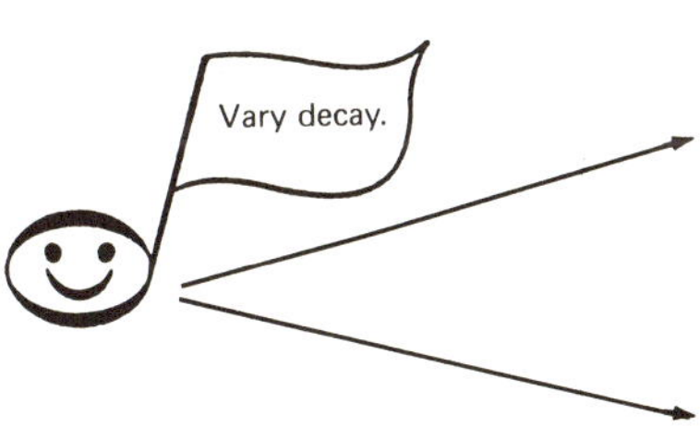


```
2Ø PRINT "THE HIGHER THE NUMBER"
3Ø PRINT "THE SLOWER THE DECAY"
4Ø PRINT "WHAT VALUE FOR DECAY"

5Ø INPUT A
3ØØ REM ** DECAY LOOP
31Ø FOR L=15 TO Ø STEP -1
32Ø SOUND Ø,121,1Ø,L
35Ø REM ** PAUSE
36Ø FOR P=1 TO A
37Ø NEXT P

39Ø NEXT L
```

Now delete all the lines of this program up to line 3ØØ by typing each line number and then pressing RETURN. Change line 360 to:

```
36Ø FOR P=1 TO 1Ø
```

Figure 5–4 Fast Attack–Slow Decay

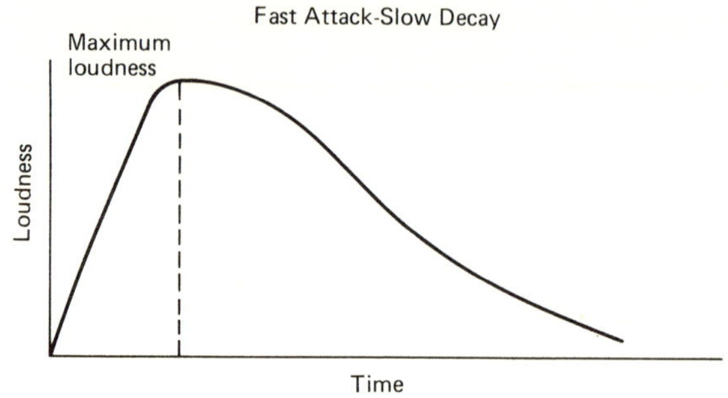

Keep lines 300 through 390 for the next section though. Here's what you should have:

```
300 REM ** DECAY LOOP
310 FOR L=15 TO 0 STEP -1
320 SOUND 0,121,10,L

350 REM ** PAUSE
360 FOR P=1 TO A
370 NEXT P

390 NEXT L
```

Attack and Decay on the Same Note

Just as you used back-to-back FOR-NEXT loops to create a rising and falling pitch in the same program, you can affect the attack and decay of the same note by simply putting attack and decay loops back-to-back in one program. If you still have lines 300 through 390 from the previous program, just add the following lines:

```
100 REM ** ATTACK LOOP
110 FOR L=0 TO 15
120 SOUND 0,121,10,L

150 REM ** PAUSE
160 FOR P=1 TO 10
170 NEXT P

190 NEXT L

200 REM ** PLAYS NOTE A WHILE
210 FOR P=1 TO 100
220 NEXT P
```

If not, simply type NEW, press RETURN, and ENTER the following program:

```
100 REM ** ATTACK LOOP
110 FOR L=0 TO 15
120 SOUND 0,121,10,L

150 REM ** PAUSE
160 FOR P=1 TO 10
170 NEXT P

190 NEXT L

200 REM ** PLAYS NOTE A WHILE
210 FOR P=1 TO 100
220 NEXT P

300 REM ** DECAY LOOP
310 FOR L=15 TO 0 STEP -1
320 SOUND 0,121,10,L
350 REM ** PAUSE
360 FOR P=1 TO 10
370 NEXT P

390 NEXT L
```

If you want to hear the note repeat, just add the following:

```
410 GOTO 110
```

Experiment with changes in lines 160 and 360 to affect the attack and decay of the note before going on to the next section.

LOUDNESS GOING BOTH WAYS

Another way to shape the note is to use two voices and have the loudness going in both directions within the same loop. ENTER and RUN the following program to hear how this affects the shape of the note:

```
1ØØ REM ** LOUDNESS GOES BOTH WAYS
11Ø FOR L=Ø TO 15
12Ø SOUND Ø,121,1Ø,L
13Ø SOUND 1,121,1Ø,15-L

2ØØ REM ** CHANGES SHAPE OF NOTE
21Ø FOR P=1 TO 1Ø
22Ø NEXT P

25Ø NEXT L
```

Try some variations in the length of the pause in line 15Ø on your own.

Many of the changes we've been making in the attack and decay of the note are very subtle. They are worth exploring both to increase your knowledge of ATARI BASIC and to better understand the nature of sound.

YOUR OWN SONG

In the remainder of this chapter, we'll build a program in which you can combine a number of the techniques you've learned for manipulating sound with ATARI BASIC. We will structure the program so that you can add and subtract blocks or *routines* of your own.

To begin, let's work with a program similar to the one at the end of the last chapter which uses READ and DATA statements to play a melody.

```
1 REM ** YOUR OWN SONG

1ØØ REM ** READS THE NOTE
12Ø READ N
22Ø SOUND Ø,N,1Ø,1Ø

31Ø FOR P=1 TO 1ØØ
32Ø NEXT P

5ØØ REM ** PLAYS NEXT NOTE

91Ø GOTO 12Ø

111Ø DATA 121,81,96,6Ø,64
112Ø DATA 35,45,64,1Ø8,121
```

ENTER and RUN this program. It's a little different in structure from the version in Chapter 4 (there are no graphics and some of the line numbers are slightly different), but it is still YOUR OWN SONG.

Restore Data and Repeat the Melody

Now that you've become familiar with FOR-NEXT loops, here's a way to RESTORE DATA and READ the melody repeatedly instead of just once. You'll also finally be able to stop getting the same ERROR message you get every time you RUN the program above. Add these lines:

```
110 FOR CYCLE=1 TO 10

510 NEXT CYCLE
520 RESTORE
910 GOTO 110
```

Line 510 replaces the GOTO statement that was there. Line 910 sends us to line 110 instead. Here's the complete listing:

```
1 REM ** YOUR OWN SONG

100 REM ** READS THE NOTE
110 FOR CYCLE=1 TO 10
120 READ N
220 SOUND 0,N,10,10

310 FOR P=1 TO 100
320 NEXT P

500 REM ** PLAYS NEXT NOTE
510 NEXT CYCLE
520 RESTORE

910 GOTO 110

1110 DATA 121,81,96,60,64
1120 DATA 35,45,64,108,121
```

Counts ten note values in DATA statements (lines 110 and 510)

Lets you use the same DATA over again (line 520)

RUN the program like this, and you'll hear the melody repeat.

We want to count ten notes in the DATA table in lines 1110 and 1120. This is done with the FOR-NEXT CYCLE loop in lines 110 through 510.

Each time through the cycle, another note value is read from the DATA table and played in the SOUND statement in line 220. Lines 310 and 320 keep the note on briefly and then the next note is read, and so on until the cycle has been completed ten times. In this way, it reads the ten note values in the DATA table.

If you have the cycle play only five times:

```
11Ø FOR CYCLE=1 TO 5
```

it will play the first five notes over and over. The cycle must be repeated once for each piece of DATA (in this case note values).

If you made line 11Ø:

```
11Ø FOR CYCLE=1 TO 15
```

it will play the first ten notes, and you'll get an out-of-data error (ERROR –6 AT LINE 12Ø).

The READ statement (line 12Ø), the SOUND statement (line 22Ø), and the pause loop (lines 31Ø and 32Ø) should all be within the FOR-NEXT CYCLE loop (lines 11Ø through 51Ø).

Change Decay of Notes Within READ-DATA Melody

Now let's change the decay of the notes as they are played. First make the pause much shorter. Change line 31Ø to:

```
31Ø FOR P=1 TO 5
```

Now add:

```
2ØØ REM ** DECAY
21Ø SOUND Ø,N,1Ø,L
39Ø NEXT L
```

You can change the decay by changing line 31Ø if you wish, or you can completely replace the decay loop (lines 2ØØ through 39Ø) with an attack loop, by making line 21Ø:

```
21Ø FOR L=15 TO Ø STEP -1
```

Other possibilities might be:

- Attack and decay on the same note.
- Loudness going both ways.

Try to replace the decay loop we've used with one or more of these. Be sure that any loop you use to change the shape of the notes occurs within the FOR-NEXT CYCLE and begins after the READ statement, and that all loops are properly nested.

You could also include a loop for ascending or descending pitch within the FOR-NEXT CYCLE loop, but the nesting gets a little tricky. Try it if you wish.

We've chosen to have a descending pitch loop outside the FOR-NEXT CYCLE loop and after the RESTORE statement in line 520, like this:

```
600 REM ** DESCENDING PITCH
610 FOR N=0 TO 255
620 SOUND 0,N,10,10
630 NEXT N

910 GOTO 110
```

After adding lines 600 through 610 above, RUN the program and you should hear the melody played. You then hear the descending pitch cycle you learned at the beginning of the chapter.

Finally add:

```
7ØØ REM ** BIRDS
71Ø FOR CYCLE=1 TO 12
72Ø FOR N=Ø TO 1Ø
73Ø SOUND Ø,N,1Ø,1Ø
74Ø NEXT N
75Ø NEXT CYCLE
```

to get this listing:

```
1 REM ** YOUR OWN SONG

1ØØ REM ** READS THE NOTE
11Ø FOR CYCLE=1 TO 1Ø
12Ø READ N

2ØØ REM ** DECAY LOOP
21Ø FOR L=15 TO Ø STEP -1
22Ø SOUND Ø,N,1Ø,L

31Ø FOR P=1 TO 5
32Ø NEXT P

39Ø NEXT L
5ØØ REM ** PLAYS NEXT NOTE
51Ø NEXT CYCLE
52Ø RESTORE

6ØØ REM ** DESCENDING PITCH
61Ø FOR N=Ø TO 255
62Ø SOUND Ø,N,1Ø,1Ø
63Ø NEXT N

7ØØ REM ** BIRDS
71Ø FOR CYCLE=1 TO 12
72Ø FOR N=Ø TO 1Ø
73Ø SOUND Ø,N,1Ø,1Ø
74Ø NEXT N
75Ø NEXT CYCLE

91Ø GOTO 11Ø

111Ø DATA 121,81,96,6Ø,64
112Ø DATA 35,45,64,1Ø8,121
```

This is a nested loop that plays a high, descending pitch (lines 720 through 740). This is repeated twelve times by the FOR-NEXT CYCLE loop in lines 710 through 750. When you RUN the program after adding these lines, you'll hear an example of how sound effects can follow one after the other.

Now add a sound effect of your own beginning at line 800. Spend some time practicing the art of moving different routines around by deleting some of the routines we've used and replacing them with your own routines.

In the next chapter you will learn to make these into subroutines to be called upon at different places in a program.

Self-Test

1. To play note values from 50 through 100, what should you make line 110 below?

```
110____________________
120 SOUND 0,N,10,10
130 NEXT N
```

2. To count by 5's, what must you do to line 110?

```
110 FOR N=0 TO 100
```

3. How would you count by 5's backwards in the same program?
4. What's wrong with the following program?

```
110 FOR L=15 TO 0 STEP -1
120 SOUND 0,121,10,L
125 FOR P=1 TO 500
130 NEXT L
150 NEXT P
```

5. What's the easiest way to delete a line from a program?
6. The way in which a note begins is called its________________.
7. What does this loop affect?

```
110 FOR L=15 TO 0 STEP -1
120 SOUND 0,121,10,L
130 NEXT L
```

8. What command allows you to reuse the same DATA in a program?

Answers

1. Line 11Ø becomes:

```
11Ø FOR N=5Ø TO 1ØØ
```

2. Line 11Ø is changed to:

```
11Ø FOR N=1ØØ TO Ø STEP -1
```

3. Make line 11Ø:

```
FOR N=1ØØ TO Ø STEP -5
```

4. The pause loop is not properly nested within the loudness loop.
5. Type the line number for the line you wish to delete and then press RETURN.
6. Attack
7. The decay of the note
8. RESTORE

Challenges

1. Write a program with a very slow attack that allows you to INPUT tone as a variable.
2. Write a program using four voices where two voices stay the same.

CHAPTER SIX

Subroutines for Graphics and Sound

In this chapter you will learn about graphic modes without text windows. You will also learn to use FOR-NEXT loops to create various graphics effects and how to make subroutines.

GRAPHIC MODES WITHOUT TEXT WINDOW

The graphics modes we have used so far (3–7) have had a text window at the bottom of the screen.

If you wish to use a graphics mode with exactly the same size plot points but without a text window, add sixteen to whatever you are using:

with text window: GRAPHICS 3
without text window: GRAPHICS 19 }
or 3 + 16
with text window: GRAPHICS 7
without text window: GRAPHICS 23 }
or 7 + 16

ENTER and RUN the following short program to plot a point in graphics mode 19, which has no text window:

```
1ØØ REM ** NO TEXT WINDOW
11Ø GRAPHICS 19
12Ø COLOR 1

2ØØ REM ** PLOTS DOT
21Ø PLOT 5,5

5ØØ REM ** WAITS HERE
51Ø GOTO 51Ø
```

RUN this program to see what happens. The screen should look like this:

The computer plots the same point that it would if you had used graphics mode 3, but there's no text window.

You may recall that the maximum number of rows available in graphics mode 3 was twenty (numbered Ø through 19). Using graphics mode 19 instead gives you four more rows in which to plot points. The number of columns is the same. Graphics mode 19 has:

4Ø columns (Ø–39)
24 rows (Ø–23)

Now let's use these limits to plot points in each corner of the screen with graphics mode 19. To do this, first change line 21Ø to:

Upper left corner → `21Ø PLOT Ø,Ø`

Remember this can be done by simply typing the new line and pressing RETURN.

Then add these lines:

Upper right corner → `22Ø PLOT 39,Ø`

Lower right corner → `23Ø PLOT 39,23`

Lower left corner → `24Ø PLOT Ø,23`

Your complete listing should now look like this:

```
1ØØ REM ** NO TEXT WINDOW
11Ø GRAPHICS 19
12Ø COLOR 1

2ØØ REM ** PLOTS DOT
21Ø PLOT 5,5
22Ø PLOT 39,Ø
23Ø PLOT 39,23
24Ø PLOT Ø,23

5ØØ REM ** WAITS HERE
51Ø GOTO 51Ø
```

You'll see more of these graphics modes without text windows in this chapter. Try some other graphics modes without text windows on your own.

PLOT POINTS WITH NESTED FOR-NEXT LOOPS

Let's make use of the concept of nested FOR-NEXT loops, which you learned in Chapter 5, to plot points in several columns and rows. Just replace lines 210 through 240 of your program with these lines:

```
21Ø FOR X=Ø TO 39 STEP 5
21Ø FOR Y=Ø TO 23 STEP 5
23Ø PLOT X,Y
24Ø NEXT Y
25Ø NEXT X
```

Your complete listing should now be:

```
1 REM ** COLOR DOTS
5Ø GRAPHICS 19

1ØØ REM ** CHANGES COLORS
12Ø COLOR 1

2ØØ REM ** PLOTS DOTS
21Ø FOR X=Ø TO 39 STEP 5
22Ø FOR Y=Ø TO 23 STEP 5
23Ø PLOT X,Y
24Ø NEXT Y
25Ø NEXT X

5ØØ REM ** STARTS AGAIN
51Ø GOTO 12Ø
```

Now RUN the program and the screen should look like this:

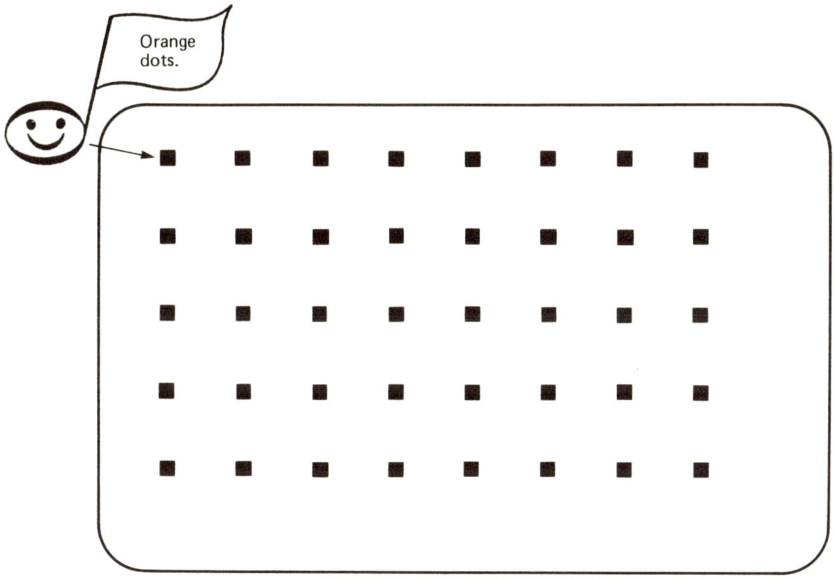

Changing the value of the STEP function in lines 210 and 220 will change the pattern of dots that appear on the screen. Can you think of a way to make these changes using an INPUT statement?

See what happens if you remove the STEP function from one of the lines and then from both lines.

CHANGE COLOR OF DOTS

Let's nest these loops within yet another loop to change the color of the dots. First, add these lines:

```
100 REM ** CHANGE COLORS
110 FOR C=1 TO 3

400 REM ** PICKS ANOTHER COLOR
410 NEXT C
```

and change line 120 to:

```
120 COLOR C
```

Finally, line 510 needs to be made:

```
510 GOTO 110
```

By now we assume you know that REM statements are always optional when adding new lines to a program.

The program listing should look like this:

```
1 REM ** COLOR DOTS
5Ø GRAPHICS 19

1ØØ REM ** CHANGES COLORS
11Ø FOR C=1 TO 3
12Ø COLOR C

2ØØ REM ** PLOTS DOTS
21Ø FOR X=Ø TO 39 STEP 5
22Ø FOR Y=Ø TO 24 STEP 5
23Ø PLOT X,Y
24Ø NEXT Y
25Ø NEXT X

4ØØ REM ** PICKS ANOTHER COLOR
41Ø NEXT C

5ØØ REM ** STARTS AGAIN
51Ø GOTO 11Ø
```

ENTER and RUN this program and you'll see the colors continually go from orange to yellow, to green, and then to orange again, and so on. This occurs as rapid waves going across the screen.

We didn't use COLOR Ø in line 11Ø of the program because we didn't want to erase the dots. Try having line 11Ø count from Ø through 3 to see what happens.

A SUBROUTINE TO PLOT THE DOTS

In this chapter and in Chapter 5, you've been learning a lot about constructing routines to manipulate sound and graphics. Often you will want a particular routine to be repeated at various times during the RUN of a program. A convenient way to accomplish this is to make that routine a *subroutine*.

Although it isn't absolutely necessary, it's generally a good idea to put subroutines after the main body of the program. The following program makes a subroutine out of a section of the "Color Dots" program above that plots the dots:

```
1 REM ** COLOR DOTS
5Ø GRAPHICS 19

1ØØ REM ** CHANGES COLORS
11Ø FOR C=1 TO 3
12Ø COLOR C

2ØØ REM ** USES SUBROUTINE
21Ø GOSUB 2Ø1Ø

4ØØ REM ** PICKS ANOTHER COLOR
41Ø NEXT C

5ØØ REM ** STARTS AGAIN
51Ø GOTO 11Ø

2ØØØ REM ** PLOTS DOTS - SUBROUTINE
2Ø1Ø FOR X=2 TO 37 STEP 5
2Ø2Ø FOR Y=Ø TO 23 STEP 5
2Ø3Ø PLOT X,Y
2Ø8Ø NEXT Y
2Ø9Ø NEXT X

21ØØ REM ** PICKS UP AFTER GOSUB
211Ø RETURN
```

AN EASY WAY TO CHANGE LINE NUMBERS

If you don't want to do a lot of extra typing, you can change the number of a program line by typing the new line number over the old line number and pressing RETURN. For example, to make line 2ØØØ out of this line:

```
2ØØ PLOT DOTS
```

use the CTRL key and the arrow keys as described in Chapter 1 to move the cursor until it covers the 2, like this:

Cursor ——→ [2]ØØ PLOT POINTS

Now type 2ØØØ and press RETURN.

You will now have both of these lines in your listing:

```
2ØØ REM ** PLOT DOTS
.
.
.
.
.
.
2ØØØ REM ** PLOT DOTS
```

Delete line 2ØØ by typing 2ØØ and pressing RETURN. If you still have the "Color Dots" program without a subroutine, change lines 21Ø through 24Ø to 2Ø1Ø through 2Ø4Ø in this way.

If you get hung up trying to do this, you can always retype the new lines (2Ø1Ø through 2Ø4Ø) and delete the old ones (21Ø through 24Ø).

In whatever way it's easiest for you, make sure you have the listing we've shown above, and then RUN the program. It does just what it did before; that is, it plots the dots and then sends waves of color through them. The way the present program does this is a little different though.

In this version, instead of having the loop that plots the dots nested within the loops to change colors (lines 11Ø through 41Ø), we've placed it at the end of the program beginning at line 2Ø1Ø, or as a subroutine.

When the program runs, a value is picked in line 11Ø and entered in the COLOR statement in line 12Ø. As the name would imply, the GOSUB statement at line 21Ø takes us out of the main body of the program and sends us to line 2Ø1Ø. The computer then executes line 2Ø1Ø and all the lines that follow, until it reaches the RETURN statement in line 211Ø. As the name of that statement would imply, it tells the computer to return to the main body of the program. It always returns to the program line immediately after the GOSUB statement. In this case it returns to line 4ØØ, which the computer ignores since it is a REM statement. So it actually picks up at line 41Ø, which completes the COLOR Loop in lines 11Ø through 41Ø.

Each time the computer gets to the GOSUB statement in line 21Ø, it executes the entire subroutine to plot dots as though it were still nested within the FOR-NEXT loop for color.

Now let's look at some ways to execute routines within the main body of the program and then occasionally use the subroutine again. For example, suppose you want to overlay another figure on the screen while the dots are still there (and then have the dots blink off and on each time they change colors).

First add these lines to draw a figure:

```
3ØØ REM ** MORE LINES
31Ø DRAWTO 2,Ø
32Ø DRAWTO 37,Ø
33Ø DRAWTO 37,2Ø
34Ø DRAWTO 2,2Ø
35Ø DRAWTO 2,Ø
```

If you've been experimenting with adding COLOR Ø in line 11Ø, make sure 11Ø is:

```
11Ø FOR C=1 TO 3
```

The complete listing should now be:

```
1 REM ** FIGURE OVERLAYS DOTS
5Ø GRAPHICS 19

1ØØ REM ** CHANGES COLORS
11Ø FOR C=1 TO 3
12Ø COLOR C

2ØØ REM ** USES SUBROUTINE
21Ø GOSUB 2Ø1Ø

3ØØ REM ** MORE LINES
31Ø DRAWTO 2,Ø
32Ø DRAWTO 37,Ø
33Ø DRAWTO 37,2Ø
34Ø DRAWTO 2,2Ø
35Ø DRAWTO 2,Ø

4ØØ REM ** PICKS ANOTHER COLOR
41Ø NEXT C

5ØØ REM ** STARTS AGAIN
51Ø GOTO 11Ø

2ØØØ REM ** PLOTS DOTS – SUBROUTINE
2Ø1Ø FOR X=2 TO 37 STEP 5
2Ø2Ø FOR Y=Ø TO 23 STEP 5
2Ø3Ø PLOT X,Y
2Ø8Ø NEXT Y
2Ø9Ø NEXT X

21ØØ REM ** PICKS UP AFTER GOSUB
211Ø RETURN
```

Plots dots first

Then draws figure

ENTER and RUN the program and you'll get this on the screen, with the colors changing as they did before.

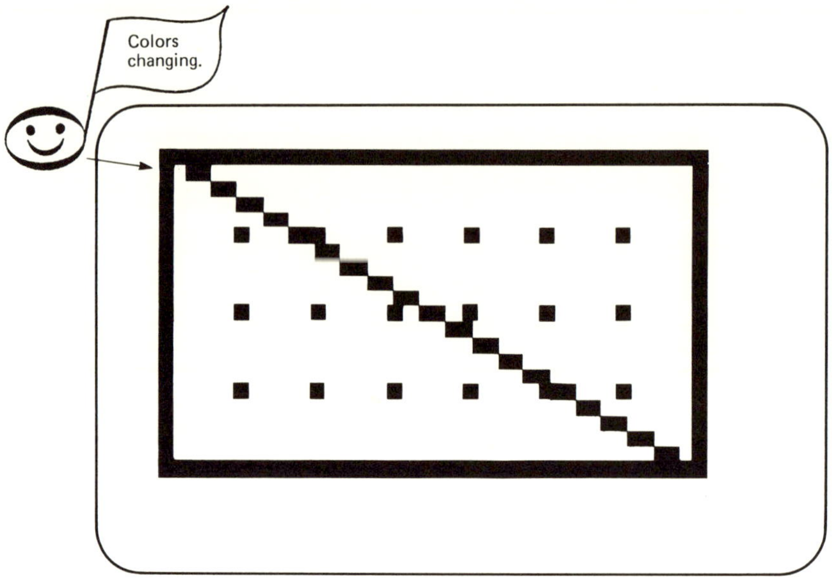

Notice that the color of the dots changes just an instant before the figure. After each new color is selected in line 12Ø, the GOSUB statement in line 21Ø plots the dots in that color before the figure is drawn in the new color at line 31Ø.

Also notice that we've begun the routine to draw the figures with DRAWTO statements at line 31Ø. If you look carefully at lines 2Ø1Ø and 2Ø2Ø in the subroutine, you'll see that the last point it plots is at column 37, row 2Ø, at the bottom right corner of the screen. The RETURN statement then brings us back to line 31Ø, which draws a line from the dot in the bottom right corner of the screen to the dot in the upper left corner of the screen. That's the diagonal in the figure. The next four DRAWTO statements (lines 31Ø through 35Ø) draw the border by drawing clockwise from one corner dot to the next.

ERASE THE DOTS WHILE THE FIGURE STAYS

Now we can take advantage of the subroutine to erase the dots while the figure stays on the screen. Just add the following lines:

```
36Ø REM ** ERASE DOTS
37Ø COLOR Ø
38Ø GOSUB 2Ø1Ø
```

The listing now should be:

```
1 REM ** COLOR DOTS
5Ø GRAPHICS 19

1ØØ REM ** CHANGES COLORS
11Ø FOR C=1 TO 3
12Ø COLOR C

2ØØ REM ** USES SUBROUTINE
21Ø GOSUB 2Ø1Ø

3ØØ REM ** MORE LINES
31Ø DRAWTO 2,Ø
32Ø DRAWTO 37,Ø
33Ø DRAWTO 37,2Ø
34Ø DRAWTO 2,2Ø
35Ø DRAWTO 2,Ø
36Ø REM ** ERASE DOTS
37Ø COLOR Ø
38Ø GOSUB 2Ø1Ø

4ØØ REM ** PICKS ANOTHER COLOR
41Ø NEXT C

5ØØ REM ** STARTS AGAIN
51Ø GOTO 11Ø

2ØØØ REM ** PLOTS DOTS - SUBROUTINE
2Ø1Ø FOR X=2 TO 37 STEP 5
2Ø2Ø FOR Y=Ø TO 23 STEP 5
2Ø3Ø PLOT X,Y
2Ø8Ø NEXT Y
2Ø9Ø NEXT X

21ØØ REM ** PICKS UP AFTER GOSUB
211Ø RETURN
```

Uses subroutine again

Now after drawing the figure, the color changes to Ø in line 37Ø and the GOSUB statement sends us down to plot all the dots in COLOR Ø. As you may recall from Chapter 2, this will erase the dots because it plots them in the same color as the background screen.

CHANGE THE FIGURE

We're going to give you one more idea that demonstrates just how much one line can sometimes change a program, and then we'll offer some suggestions on how you might explore the concepts before going on.

Take a careful look at the subroutine to plot the dots. If you put a DRAWTO statement after the PLOT statement in line 2030, but before either of the NEXT statements in lines 2080 and 2090, the machine will draw a line to whatever point you indicated after it plots each of the dots. That adds quite a few lines to the drawing. To get a sense of this, add this line to the program:

```
2050 DRAWTO 19,10
```

This tells the computer to draw a line from each point it plots to a point more or less in the center of the screen.

Since the way this new figure comes on and off the screen is a major part of the effect created by adding this line, we won't try to picture it for you. RUN the program and you'll see what we mean.

If you have an ATARI 410™ Program Recorder or an ATARI 810™ Disk Drive system, we suggest you save this program before experimenting since we will continue to build upon it in the second half of the chapter. The manual that accompanies each of these systems explains their use. We will not attempt to do so here.

IDEAS FOR EXPLORATION

Try making line 2050:

```
2050 DRAWTO A, B
```

and then add a few INPUT statements to change the location of the point to which the lines are drawn. Move line 2050 to line 2085 between the NEXT Y and NEXT X statements and explore that using INPUT statements.

NESTED SUBROUTINES

Just as you are able to nest FOR-NEXT loops within other loops, you can also nest subroutines. One subroutine is not actually placed within the other as with FOR-NEXT loops, but you can use a GOSUB statement to temporarily leave a subroutine. Take a look at the subroutine for the graphics program we've been working with in this chapter.

```
2ØØØ REM ** PLOTS DOTS – SUBROUTINE
2Ø1Ø FOR X=2 TO 37 STEP 5
2Ø2Ø FOR Y=Ø TO 23 STEP 5
2Ø3Ø PLOT X,Y
2Ø8Ø NEXT Y
2Ø9Ø NEXT X

21ØØ REM ** PICKS UP AFTER GOSUB
211Ø RETURN
```

Now, suppose you'd like to have some sounds to accompany the graphics that occur in this subroutine. Let's write a subroutine to accomplish this. First, put a GOSUB statement at line 2Ø6Ø like this:

```
2Ø6Ø GOSUB 3Ø1Ø
```

And then add these lines:

```
3ØØØ REM ** SUBROUTINE TO PLAY NOTES
3Ø1Ø FOR L=15 TO Ø STEP -5
3Ø2Ø SOUND Ø,X+Y,1Ø,L
3Ø3Ø NEXT L
3Ø4Ø RETURN
```

The listing of the two subroutines should now be:

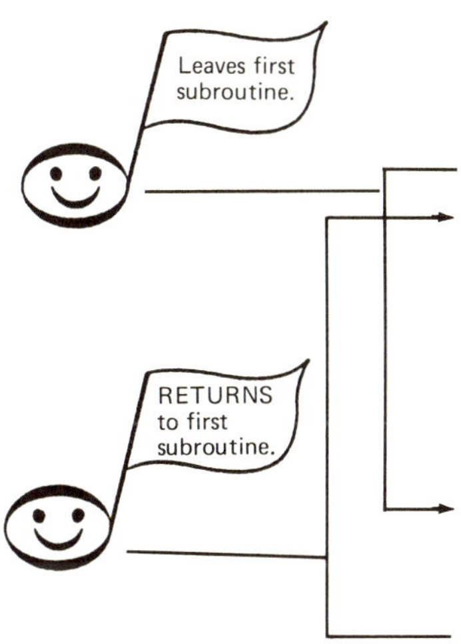


```
2ØØØ REM ** PLOTS DOTS – SUBROUTINE
2Ø1Ø FOR X=2 TO 37 STEP 5
2Ø2Ø FOR Y=Ø TO 2Ø STEP 5
2Ø3Ø PLOT X,Y
2Ø5Ø DRAWTO 19,1Ø
2Ø6Ø GOSUB 3Ø1Ø
2Ø7Ø NEXT Y
2Ø8Ø NEXT X

21ØØ REM ** PICKS UP AFTER GOSUB
211Ø RETURN

3ØØØ REM ** SUBROUTINE TO PLAY NOTES
3Ø1Ø FOR L=15 to Ø STEP -5
3Ø2Ø SOUND Ø,X+Y,1Ø,L
3Ø3Ø NEXT L
3Ø4Ø RETURN
```

The main body of the program remains the same. RUN the program and you'll hear it play a rapid sequence of notes as it is drawing the figure. It plays the note sequence again as it erases the figure, then again as it redraws the figure, and so on until you stop the run.

Each time through the FOR-NEXT loop in lines 2010 through 2110, after plotting a point and drawing a line, we come to the GOSUB statement at line 2060. This sends us to line 3010 where a note is played with decay loop. The note value used is the sum of the values of X and Y chosen in the original subroutine.

Before looking at how we've done it below, see if you can add a subroutine to play a rising pitch with note values from 50 to 0 similar to what you learned in Chapter 5. Have this occur after the figure is drawn and the notes played. HINT: The GOSUB statement to send you to the new subroutine should occur after the FOR-NEXT loops for X and Y in the original subroutine.

We added the following lines to do it:

```
2090 GOSUB 3060
```

and:

```
3050 REM ** RISING PITCH
3060 FOR N=50 TO 0 STEP -1
3070 SOUND 0,N,10,10
3080 NEXT N
3090 RETURN
```

Make sure you have the rising pitch subroutine added properly, and RUN the program. First you'll hear the note sequence played as the figure is drawn, then a whistle before it starts to erase. Once it's erased, you hear the whistle again before it draws the next figure, and so on until you stop the run.

Here's the complete listing of the program:

```
1 REM *** SOUND PATTERNS
50 GRAPHICS 19

100 REM ** CHANGES COLORS
110 FOR C=1 TO 3
120 COLOR C

200 REM ** USES SUBROUTINE
210 GOSUB 2010
```

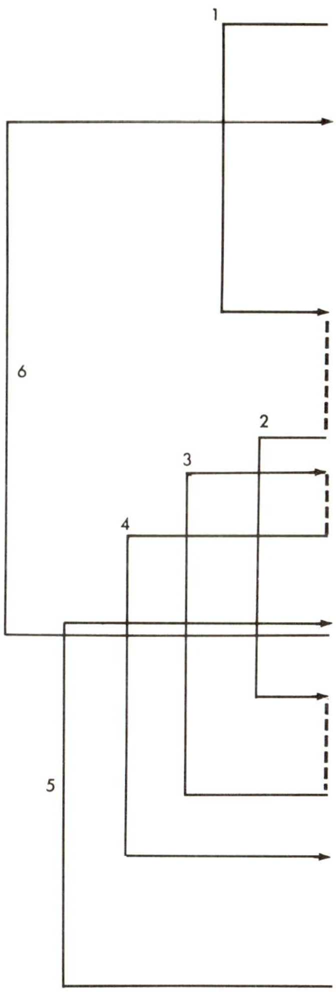


```
3ØØ REM ** MORE LINES
31Ø DRAWTO 2,Ø
32Ø DRAWTO 37,Ø
33Ø DRAWTO 37,2Ø
34Ø DRAWTO 2,2Ø
35Ø DRAWTO 2,Ø
36Ø REM ** ERASE DOTS
37Ø COLOR Ø
38Ø GOSUB 2Ø1Ø

4ØØ REM ** PICKS ANOTHER COLOR
41Ø NEXT C;

5ØØ REM ** STARTS AGAIN
51Ø GOTO 11Ø

2ØØØ REM ** PLOTS DOTS – SUBROUTINE
2Ø1Ø FOR X=2 TO 37 STEP 5
2Ø2Ø FOR Y=Ø TO 2Ø STEP 5
2Ø3Ø PLOT X,Y
2Ø5Ø DRAWTO 19,1Ø
2Ø6Ø GOSUB 3Ø1Ø
2Ø7Ø NEXT Y
2Ø8Ø NEXT X
2Ø9Ø GOSUB 3Ø6Ø

21ØØ REM ** PICKS UP AFTER GOSUB
211Ø RETURN
3ØØØ REM ** SUBROUTINE TO PLAY NOTES
3Ø1Ø FOR L=15 TO Ø STEP –5
3Ø2Ø SOUND Ø,X+Y,1Ø,L
3Ø3Ø NEXT L
3Ø4Ø RETURN

3Ø5Ø REM ** RISING PITCH
3Ø6Ø FOR N=5Ø TO Ø STEP –1
3Ø7Ø SOUND Ø,N,1Ø,1Ø
3Ø8Ø NEXT N
3Ø9Ø RETURN
```

The numbers 1 through 6 indicate the order in which program parts are executed.

You can also place a GOSUB statement in the main program to make use of this second subroutine. For example, add these lines and hear what happens when you RUN it:

```
45Ø REM *** WHISTLES 3 TIMES
46Ø FOR CYCLE = 1 TO 3
47Ø GOSUB 3Ø6Ø
48Ø NEXT CYCLE
```

Now after it has drawn and erased the figure in each color while making sounds (after it has completed the loop in lines 11Ø through 41Ø), it whistles three times before it starts again.

But what happens if you try to go from the main program to the subroutine to play notes in lines 3Ø1Ø through 3Ø4Ø, by adding a line something like:

```
49Ø GOSUB 3Ø1Ø
```

Try it and see what happens.

If you listen carefully, you'll notice that after it goes through the cycle of different colored figures and whistles three times, it plays a single note before it starts again with the sequence of drawings and sound. Since the values for X and Y in the SOUND statement in line 3Ø2Ø are taken from the subroutine in lines 2Ø1Ø through 2Ø8Ø, and we've bypassed that subroutine by coming from the main program, the computer used the last values computed for the sum of X and Y (that is, 37 + 2Ø) for a note value.

In this case it didn't add much to the program, but it didn't "crash" the program either (that is, stop and give you an ERROR message). Be careful using nested subroutines in this way because often they will create errors or "bugs" in the program.

FOR-NEXT GRAPHICS MODE

In the beginning of this chapter, we discussed how to change graphics modes 3–7 to equivalent modes without text windows. You can use a FOR-NEXT loop to change graphics modes in such a way that a figure will change size on the screen. Let's add a few final lines to the program we've been using in this chapter to do this:

```
3Ø REM *** CHANGE GRAPHICS MODE
4Ø FOR G=23 TO 19 STEP -2
5Ø GRAPHICS G

49Ø NEXT G
```

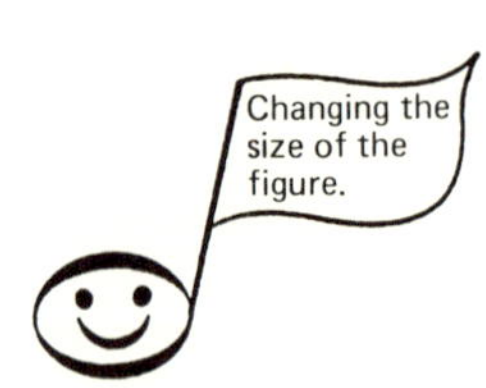

and change line 51Ø to:

```
51Ø GOTO 4Ø
```

Add these lines and RUN the program. You'll see the same cycle of colors and sounds as before, but the figure will occur in three different sizes starting in the upper right corner of the screen.

The STEP –2 in line 4Ø causes the computer to enter graphics mode 23 (equivalent to GR. 7), then Mode 21 (equivalent to GR. 5), and finally graphics mode 19 (equivalent to GR. 3). We've skipped the even numbered modes 2Ø through 22 which are equivalent to modes 4 and 6 with text windows. This is because, as we mentioned in Chapter 3, these are two-color modes and we are using four colors (Ø through 3) in this program.

You can use modes 2Ø and 22 if you wish, but these modes use only values of Ø and 1. Whenever a value of 2 is entered by the FOR-NEXT loop for COLOR in lines 11Ø through 41Ø, the compuer will treat it as though it were a Ø and erase the figure. This is called a *default*. Actually, when it sees a value of 3 for COLOR in these modes, it defaults to 1 and draws the figure in COLOR 1.

In the four-color modes (3, 5, and 7) or (19, 21, and 23) any number above 3 will default to a value of Ø, 1, 2, or 3. For example:

```
12Ø COLOR 5
```

would default to:

```
12Ø COLOR 1
```

And:

```
12Ø COLOR 11
```

would default to:

```
12Ø COLOR 3
```

The FOR-NEXT loop for graphics must completely encompass the loop for COLOR. Or to say it the other way around, the FOR-NEXT loop for COLOR must be nested within the FOR-NEXT loop for graphics.

Here's the complete listing for the program:

```
1 REM *** PATTERN SIZE CHANGES

30 REM ** CHANGE GRAPHICS MODE
40 FOR G=23 TO 19 STEP -2
50 GRAPHICS G

100 REM ** CHANGES COLORS
110 FOR C=1 TO 3
120 COLOR C

200 REM ** USES SUBROUTINE
210 GOSUB 2010

300 REM ** MORE LINES
310 DRAWTO 2,0
320 DRAWTO 37,0
330 DRAWTO 37,20
340 DRAWTO 2,20
350 DRAWTO 2,0
360 REM ** ERASE DOTS
370 COLOR 0
380 GOSUB 2010

400 REM ** PICKS ANOTHER COLOR
410 NEXT C

450 REM ** WHISTLES 3 TIMES
460 FOR CYCLE=1 TO 3
470 GOSUB 3060
480 NEXT CYCLE
490 NEXT G

500 REM ** STARTS AGAIN
510 GOTO 40

2000 REM ** PLOTS DOTS – SUBROUTINE
2010 FOR X=2 TO 37 STEP 5
2020 FOR Y=0 TO 20 STEP 5
2030 PLOT X,Y
2050 DRAWTO 19,10
2060 GOSUB 3010
2070 NEXT Y
2080 NEXT X
2090 GOSUB 3060
```

Graphics mode loop (lines 40–490)

Color loop (lines 110–410)

Whistle loop (lines 460–480)

```
2100 REM ** PICKS UP AFTER GOSUB
2110 RETURN
3000 REM ** SUBROUTINE TO PLAY NOTES
3010 FOR L=15 TO 0 STEP -5
3020 SOUND 0,X+Y,10,L
3030 NEXT L
3040 RETURN

3050 REM ** RISING PITCH
3060 FOR N=50 TO 0 STEP -1
3070 SOUND 0,N,10,10
3080 NEXT N
3090 RETURN
```

Once again, if you have an ATARI 410 Program Recorder or an ATARI 810 Disk Drive system, we suggest you save this program for later reference.

Experiment with "calling" the subroutines from a few more places in the program. Moving line 510 down to line 1010, or something similar, will give you room to add several more lines to the main program. Some possible additions are drawing and erasing another figure, introducing more sounds, and calling several new subroutines that you add to the end of the program.

As you make these explorations, you'll probably see our old friend the ERROR message now and then. Don't give up; it's rather like trying to make it across the stream and testing to see which rocks are slippery or too loose to provide footing. Fortunately, it's a shallow stream so there's no chance of drowning, and sometimes getting your feet wet is how you learn the way. Here's a chart of the columns and rows and the colors available in graphics modes 3 through 7 and 19 through 21:

Graphics Mode		Columns	Rows	Colors
3	Text window	(0–39)	(0–19)	4
19	No text window	(0–39)	(0–23)	4
4	Text window	(0–79)	(0–39)	2
20	No text window	(0–79)	(0–47)	2
5	Text window	(0–79)	(0–39)	4
21	No text window	(0–79)	(0–47)	4
6	Text window	(0–159)	(0–79)	2
22	No text window	(0–159)	(0–95)	2
7	Text window	(0–159)	(0–79)	4
23	No text window	(0–159)	(0–95)	4

In Chapter 7 you'll learn about graphics modes 8 and 24, the SETCOLOR command, and how to do "high-resolution" graphics—graphics with much smaller plot points that let you draw fine lines.

Self-Test

1. To change from a graphics mode with text window to one with the same size plot points and no text window, what number do you add?
2. What statement is used to leave the main program and execute a subroutine?
3. What's needed before these lines can function as a subroutine?

```
1Ø1Ø SOUND Ø,121,1Ø,1Ø
1Ø2Ø SOUND 1,122,1Ø,1Ø
1Ø3Ø SOUND 2,6Ø,1Ø,8
1Ø4Ø SOUND 3,61,1Ø,8
1Ø5Ø FOR P=1 TO 1ØØØ
1Ø6Ø NEXT P
```

4. Where does the RETURN statement at the end of a subroutine send you in the program?
5. What's an easy way to change line numbers with ATARI BASIC?
6. Can you leave one subroutine and execute another subroutine?
7. In a nested subroutine, where does the RETURN statement send you?
8. How many times will the subroutine be used in these lines?

```
46Ø FOR CYCLE=1 TO 3
47Ø GOSUB 3Ø6Ø
48Ø NEXT CYCLE
```

Answers

1. 16
2. A GOSUB statement
3. A RETURN statement to bring you back to the main program
4. To the program line immediately following the GOSUB statement that activated the subroutine
5. Type the new line number over the old one
6. Yes. This is called a nested subroutine.
7. Back to complete the subroutine from which you came
8. Three times

Challenges

1. In this chapter, we drew a figure on the screen and then erased it. See if you can construct a program that draws two separate figures and leaves one on the screen and erases the other, and then switches by redrawing the figure it has just erased and erasing the one it has just drawn.
2. Try adding some routines for sound to accompany each of the figures.

CHAPTER SEVEN

The Finer Points of Graphics

You've learned to use both two- and four-color graphics with and without text windows. In this chapter you will learn to use the SETCOLOR command, which gives you greater variety of options for color grahics with your ATARI Computer. You will also learn to use a high-resolution graphics mode (8 or 24). Finally, you will learn to use IF-THEN statements to have the computer select variables or execute routines.

SETCOLOR COMMAND

The SETCOLOR command has three parameters. Let's use it in a short program and then discuss its functions. ENTER and RUN the following program:

```
1 REM *** SETCOLOR

100 REM ** THE BEGINNING
110 GRAPHICS 19
120 COLOR 1

200 REM ** CHANGES COLORS
220 SETCOLOR 2,8,6
230 GOSUB 3010

500 REM ** WAITS
510 GOTO 510

3000 REM ** DRAW HEXAGRAM
3010 PLOT 10,10
3020 DRAWTO 15,5
3030 DRAWTO 25,5
3040 DRAWTO 30,10
3050 DRAWTO 25,15
3060 DRAWTO 15,15
3070 DRAWTO 10,10
4090 RETURN
```

This program is structured so that it will be easy to add more lines and routines later.

When you RUN this program, you should get an orange hexagram on the screen:

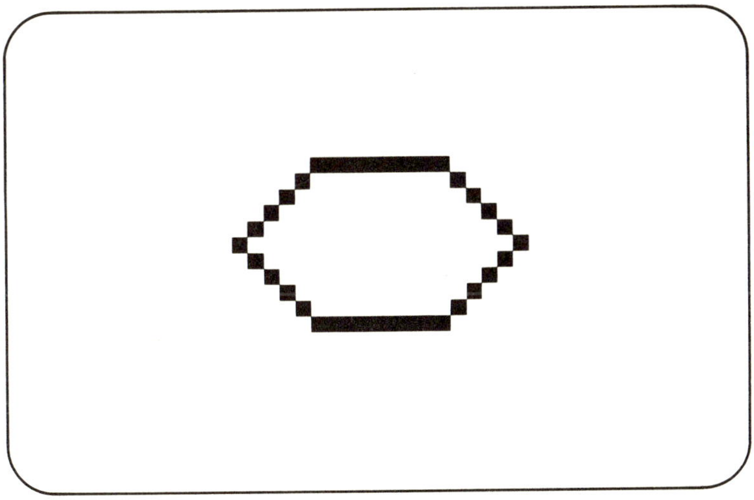

The three parameters of the SETCOLOR command are:

Color Register	(Ø through 4)
Hue	(Ø through 15)
Luminance	(Even numbers from Ø to 14)

In line 21Ø of the preceding program these are:

```
21Ø SETCOLOR 2,8,1Ø
```

Each variable in the SETCOLOR command depends upon other commands used in the program, like the graphics mode used or the value used in the COLOR command. Since these variables can be combined in so many ways, we won't try to explain what each combination does. We will demonstrate some ways to make variables of the different parameters using INPUT statements and FOR-NEXT loops so that you can explore them yourself. Appendix D shows the relationship between different COLOR commands and the SETCOLOR command for each of the graphics modes.

INPUT Color Register

Let's make use of PRINT statements to print instructions on the screen before the graphics begin. Then we'll add an INPUT statement so that we can enter different values for *color register*. Add these lines:

```
Ø REM *** SETCOLOR PARAMETERS
1 REM *** INPUT COLOR REGISTER

1Ø PRINT "ENTER Ø - 4"
2Ø PRINT "FOR COLOR REGISTER"
25 PRINT
3Ø INPUT CR
```

The extra PRINT statement at line 25 will print a blank line so that the text is easier to read when it's printed. It's not essential to the function of the program, so you don't have to use extra print statements if you don't wish. Now change line 22Ø to:

```
22Ø SETCOLOR CR,8,6
```

To save yourself having to RUN the program each time you want to INPUT a new value for color register, replace line 51Ø with:

```
51Ø FOR P=1 TO 1ØØØ
52Ø NEXT P
53Ø GOTO 1Ø
```

This will cause the hexagram to stay on the screen briefly after you INPUT a value for color register and then go back and wait for you to INPUT another variable.

Make sure you have this listing and then RUN the program:

```
Ø REM *** SETCOLOR PARAMETERS
1 REM *** INPUT COLOR REGISTER

1Ø PRINT "ENTER Ø - 4"
2Ø PRINT "FOR COLOR REGISTER"
25 PRINT
3Ø INPUT CR

1ØØ REM ** THE BEGINNING
11Ø GRAPHICS 19
12Ø COLOR 1

2ØØ REM ** CHANGES COLORS
22Ø SETCOLOR CR,8,6
23Ø GOSUB 3Ø1Ø

5ØØ REM ** WAITS
51Ø FOR P=1 TO 1ØØØ
52Ø NEXT P
53Ø GOTO 1Ø

3ØØØ REM ** DRAW HEXAGRAM
3Ø1Ø PLOT 1Ø,1Ø
3Ø2Ø DRAWTO 15,5
3Ø3Ø DRAWTO 25,5
3Ø4Ø DRAWTO 3Ø,1Ø
3Ø5Ø DRAWTO 25,15
3Ø6Ø DRAWTO 15,15
3Ø7Ø DRAWTO 1Ø,1Ø
4Ø9Ø RETURN
```

Changes color register (lines 3Ø and 22Ø)

Different values for the color register will allow you to change the hue of either the figure, the background screen, or the text window. Color register doesn't change these by itself, but determines which (figure, background, or text window) will change hue when you vary the hue parameter. For example, when you enter a value of Ø for color register, the hexagram will be blue. In COLOR 1, a value of Ø for color register allows the hue of the figure to be changed. It is actually the value 8 for hue, which changes the color.

To see this, enter a value of 4 for color register. Now the figure becomes orange and the background screen becomes blue. Orange is the "default" color for the figure. Values of 1, 2, 3, or 4 will result in an orange figure regardless of the value entered for hue.

Now try changing the graphics mode to graphics mode 3 in line 110, and you will get a light blue text window if you enter a value of 2 for color register. If you try to enter a value greater than 4 for color register, you'll "crash" the program; that is, you'll get an ERROR message and have to start the program over. Be careful, too, when running this program to wait for the prompt (question mark) to come on the screen each time before you enter another value. If you try to enter another number while the machine is pausing at lines 510 and 520, the program will crash.

We will look at the two remaining parameters in the SETCOLOR command (hue and luminance), using a constant value of 1 in the COLOR command in line 120. Be sure to try some of the experiments we suggest using different values for the COLOR command.

INPUT Hue

The second parameter in the SETCOLOR command is *hue*. It can have values for 0 through 15. To INPUT hue as a variable in the program we've been using, making the following additions and changes.
Add:

```
35 PRINT
40 PRINT "ENTER 0-15"
50 PRINT "FOR HUE"
60 INPUT H
```

and change line 220 to:

```
220 SETCOLOR CR, H, 6
```

The complete listing is:

```
Ø REM *** SETCOLOR PARAMETERS
1 REM *** INPUT COLOR REGISTER
2 REM *** INPUT HUE

1Ø PRINT "ENTER Ø - 4"
2Ø PRINT "FOR COLOR REGISTER"
25 PRINT
3Ø INPUT CR
35 PRINT
4Ø PRINT "ENTER Ø - 15"
5Ø PRINT "FOR HUE"
6Ø INPUT H

1ØØ REM ** THE BEGINNING
11Ø GRAPHICS 19
12Ø COLOR 1

2ØØ REM ** CHANGES COLORS
22Ø SETCOLOR CR,H,6
23Ø GOSUB 3Ø1Ø

5ØØ REM ** WAITS
51Ø FOR P=1 TO 1ØØØ
52Ø NEXT P
53Ø GOTO 1Ø

3ØØØ REM ** DRAW HEXAGRAM
3Ø1Ø PLOT 1Ø,1Ø
3Ø2Ø DRAWTO 15,5
3Ø3Ø DRAWTO 25,5
3Ø4Ø DRAWTO 3Ø,1Ø
3Ø5Ø DRAWTO 25,15
3Ø6Ø DRAWTO 15,15
3Ø7Ø DRAWTO 1Ø,1Ø
4Ø9Ø RETURN
```

When you RUN this program, values of 1, 2, or 3 for color register will default to an orange figure with no color background, regardless of the value used for hue. A value of Ø for color register will allow you to change the hue of the figure with the second variable you INPUT. The background screen remains gray.

If you use a value of 4 in the color register parameter, changing the hue parameter will affect the color of the background screen, while the figure stays orange.

Now change line 11Ø to:

```
11Ø GRAPHICS 3
```

and then experiment with changes in hue in each of the five color registers (Ø–4).

Which value for hue allows you to change:

- The hue of the figure?
- The hue of the background screen?
- The hue of the text window?

Which values for color register will default to an orange figure with no changes in hue?

To better understand these relationships, look up graphics mode 3 in Appendix D, and go down column 1 to COLOR 1.

INPUT Color Luminance

The third variable in the SETCOLOR command is the *color luminance;* this affects the amount of brightness in either the figure or the background, depending on the color register used. To explore the relationship between all three parameters of the SETCOLOR command, add these lines to the program:

```
65 PRINT
7Ø PRINT "ENTER EVEN NUMBER (Ø–14)"
8Ø PRINT "FOR LUMINANCE"
9Ø INPUT LU
```

and change line 22Ø to:

```
22Ø SETCOLOR CR,H,LU
```

Here's the complete listing:

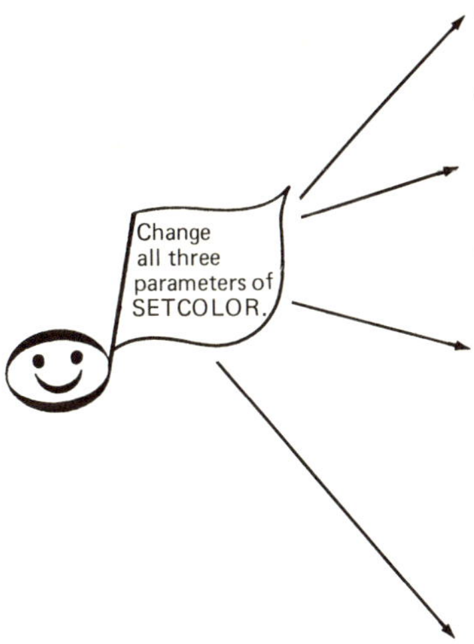


```
Ø REM *** SETCOLOR PARAMETERS
1 REM *** INPUT ALL

1Ø PRINT "ENTER Ø–4"
2Ø PRINT "FOR COLOR REGISTER"
3Ø INPUT CR
35 PRINT
4Ø PRINT "ENTER Ø–15"
5Ø PRINT "FOR HUE"
6Ø INPUT H
65 PRINT
7Ø PRINT "ENTER EVEN NUMBER (Ø–14)"
8Ø PRINT "FOR LUMINANCE"
9Ø INPUT LU

1ØØ REM ** THE BEGINNING
11Ø GRAPHICS 19
12Ø COLOR 1

2ØØ REM ** CHANGES COLORS
22Ø SETCOLOR CR,H,LU
23Ø GOSUB 3Ø1Ø

5ØØ REM ** WAITS
51Ø FOR P=1 TO 1ØØØ
52Ø NEXT P
53Ø GOTO 1Ø

3ØØØ REM ** DRAW HEXAGRAM
3Ø1Ø PLOT 1Ø,1Ø
3Ø2Ø DRAWTO 15,5
3Ø3Ø DRAWTO 25,5
3Ø4Ø DRAWTO 3Ø,1Ø
3Ø5Ø DRAWTO 25,15
3Ø6Ø DRAWTO 15,15
3Ø7Ø DRAWTO 1Ø,1Ø
4Ø9Ø RETURN
```

RUN the program and try many combinations of the variables. Remember, values of 1, 2, or 3 for color register (the first variable you INPUT) will default to an orange figure and won't be affected by hue or color luminance. So INPUT Ø or 4 for color register. Also be sure to explore the results of changing the value for COLOR in line 12Ø.

Be careful not to crash the program by trying to enter a variable while the figure is on the screen or by trying to enter an incorrect value for one of the parameters. These concepts will take some time to fully grasp. Careful study of Appendix D should be helpful.

FOR-NEXT HUE

The parameters of the SETCOLOR command can also be changed with a FOR-NEXT loop similar to the way in which you changed the parameters of the SOUND statement in Chapter 5. For example, let's use a FOR-NEXT loop to change the values for hue in the figure we've been using. We can rebuild the previous program by doing some deleting and changing.

First, delete all lines up to line 11Ø.

Also delete lines 5ØØ through 53Ø.

Now add lines:

```
21Ø FOR H=Ø TO 15
```

and:

```
23Ø NEXT H
```

Also add:

```
5ØØ ** STARTS LOOP AGAIN
51Ø GOTO 21Ø
```

And finally change line 22Ø to:

```
22Ø SETCOLOR Ø,H,6
```

It may be just as easy for you to type NEW and start over. However you accomplish it, make sure you have this listing:

```
1ØØ REM ** THE BEGINNING
11Ø GRAPHICS 19
12Ø COLOR 1

2ØØ REM ** CHANGES HUES
21Ø FOR H=Ø TO 15
22Ø SETCOLOR CR,H,6
23Ø GOSUB 3Ø1Ø
29Ø NEXT H

5ØØ REM ** STARTS LOOP AGAIN
51Ø GOTO 15Ø

3ØØØ REM ** DRAW HEXAGRAM
3Ø1Ø PLOT 1Ø,1Ø
3Ø2Ø DRAWTO 15,5
3Ø3Ø DRAWTO 25,5
3Ø4Ø DRAWTO 3Ø,1Ø
3Ø5Ø DRAWTO 25,15
3Ø6Ø DRAWTO 15,15
3Ø7Ø DRAWTO 1Ø,1Ø
4Ø9Ø RETURN
```

Now RUN the program and you should see the figure appear on the screen, continually changing colors.

Each time through the loop in lines 21Ø through 29Ø the machine ENTERs a value for hue in line 22Ø and then uses the subroutine to draw the figure. When all sixteen values for hue have been used, line 51Ø sends us back to start the loop again.

Hue changes happen pretty fast this way, so if you want to see each hue a little more distinctly, you can add a pause each time the figure is drawn with these lines.

Add these lines and RUN the program to pause at each hue.

```
3Ø8Ø FOR P=1 TO 1ØØ
3Ø9Ø NEXT P
```

We've put the pause inside the subroutine. It would have the same effect if you put it inside the FOR-NEXT loop for hue, for example, at lines 24Ø and 25Ø. Either way will result in a pause after each hue has been entered. If you put the pause outside of the loop, for example, at line 41Ø, the machine will RUN through all sixteen hues without pausing and pause only at the last value for hue, that is 15. So if you want to see each hue distinctly, you must put the pause within the loop.

Here's a complete listing of the program with the pause in the subroutine:

```
100 REM ** THE BEGINNING
110 GRAPHICS 19
120 COLOR 1

200 REM ** CHANGES HUES
210 FOR H=0 TO 15
220 SETCOLOR CR,H,6
230 GOSUB 3010
290 NEXT H

500 REM ** STARTS LOOP AGAIN
510 GOTO 150

3000 REM ** DRAW HEXAGRAM
3010 PLOT 10,10
3020 DRAWTO 15,5
3030 DRAWTO 25,5
3040 DRAWTO 30,10
3050 DRAWTO 25,15
3060 DRAWTO 15,15
3070 DRAWTO 10,10
3080 FOR P=1 TO 100
3090 NEXT P
4090 RETURN
```

Pauses each time the figure is drawn → (lines 3080–3090)

Change Hue of Figure and Background

You can also use a FOR-NEXT loop to change the color register, but since values of 1 through 3 for color register will default to orange, you'll get the most dramatic effect by using a STEP function to count just 0 and 4 in the color register loop.

Add these lines to change color register with a FOR-NEXT loop:

```
150 FOR CR=0 TO 4 STEP 4
```

and:

```
350 NEXT CR
```

This will nest the FOR-NEXT loop for hue within the color register loop. Finally, change line 220 to:

```
SETCOLOR CR,H,6
```

The complete listing is:

```
Ø REM **** DOUBLE LOOPS

1ØØ REM ** CHANGES COLOR REGISTER
11Ø GRAPHICS 19
12Ø COLOR 1
15Ø FOR CR=Ø TO 4 STEP 4

2ØØ REM ** CHANGES HUES
21Ø FOR H=Ø TO 15
22Ø SETCOLOR CR,H,6
23Ø GOSUB 3Ø1Ø
29Ø NEXT H
35Ø NEXT CR

5ØØ REM ** STARTS LOOP AGAIN
51Ø GOTO 15Ø

3ØØØ REM ** DRAW HEXAGRAM
3Ø1Ø PLOT 1Ø,1Ø
3Ø2Ø DRAWTO 15,5
3Ø3Ø DRAWTO 25,5
3Ø4Ø DRAWTO 3Ø,1Ø
3Ø5Ø DRAWTO 25,15
3Ø6Ø DRAWTO 15,15
3Ø7Ø DRAWTO 1Ø,1Ø
3Ø8Ø FOR P=1 TO 1ØØ
3Ø9Ø NEXT P
4Ø9Ø RETURN
```

RUN this program to see the figures and the background change hue.

In the next section we're going to build on the "Changing Hues" program that appeared earlier. You can either retype the program or make the following changes and deletions.

Delete lines 14Ø and 15Ø.
Delete line 35Ø.
Delete lines 3Ø8Ø and 3Ø9Ø.
Change line 22Ø to:

```
22Ø SETCOLOR Ø,H,6
```

Make any other changes you need to come up with this listing:

```
100 REM *** CHANGING HUES
110 GRAPHICS 19
120 COLOR 1

200 REM ** CHANGES COLORS
210 FOR H=0 TO 15
220 SETCOLOR 0,H,6
230 GOSUB 3010
290 NEXT H

500 REM ** STARTS LOOP AGAIN
510 GOTO 210

3000 REM ** DRAW HEXAGRAM
3010 PLOT 10,10
3020 DRAWTO 15,5
3030 DRAWTO 25,5
3040 DRAWTO 30,10
3050 DRAWTO 25,15
3060 DRAWTO 15,15
3070 DRAWTO 10,10
4090 RETURN
```

MOVING THE FIGURE

Suppose you were creating a game in which you wanted to use a figure like the one in the program we've been using as a star ship that could be moved around on the screen. Obviously you don't want to type in a whole routine every time the figure is to move. You can save yourself the trouble by entering variables for the intial plot point in line 3010 and then having the DRAWTO statements in lines 3020 change in relationship to these variables.

For example, change line 3010 to:

```
3010 PLOT X,Y
```

Now assume for a moment that X and Y are still 10 and 10. Looking at line 3020 you can see that the values for column and row in the DRAWTO statement can be changed to X + 5 (10 + 5) for column and Y – 5 (10 – 5) for row. So line 3020 becomes:

```
3020 DRAWTO X+5, Y-5
```

In the same way, lines 3030 through 3070 can be changed to:

```
3Ø3Ø DRAWTO X+5,Y–5
3Ø4Ø DRAWTO X+2Ø,Y
3Ø5Ø DRAWTO X+15,Y+5
3Ø6Ø DRAWTO X+5,Y+5
3Ø7Ø DRAWTO X,Y
3Ø8Ø GOSUB 5Ø1Ø
4Ø9Ø RETURN
```

To provide room to move the figure around, let's change line 110 to:

```
11Ø GRAPHICS 23
```

The program isn't quite ready to RUN yet. We need to have a way to ENTER values for X and Y. Add the following lines to allow you to INPUT these values:

```
1Ø PRINT "ENTER – 139 FOR ROW"
2Ø INPUT X
3Ø PRINT
5Ø PRINT "ENTER 5 – 9Ø FOR ROW"
6Ø INPUT Y
```

The complete listing should now be:

```
0 REM *** MOVING STAR SHIP

10 PRINT "ENTER – 139 FOR ROW"
20 INPUT X
30 PRINT
50 PRINT "ENTER 5 – 90 FOR ROW"
60 INPUT Y

100 REM ** SETUP FOR GRAPHICS
110 GRAPHICS 23
120 COLOR 1

200 REM ** CHANGES HUES
210 FOR H=0 TO 15
220 SETCOLOR 0,H,12
260 GOSUB 3010
290 NEXT H

500 REM ** STARTS LOOP AGAIN
510 GOTO 10

3000 REM ** DRAW STAR SHIP
3010 PLOT X,Y
3020 DRAWTO X+5,Y–5
3030 DRAWTO X+15,Y–5
3040 DRAWTO X+20,Y
3050 DRAWTO X+15,Y+5
3060 DRAWTO X+5,Y+5
3070 DRAWTO X,Y
4090 RETURN
```

Notice that, although graphics mode 23 has columns from 0 through 159, we've indicated in the PRINT statement in line 10 that you should not exceed a value of 139 for column. This is because in line 3040 of the subroutine to draw the figure, we will have a value of 139 + 20 = 159 if we INPUT 139 for column. Likewise, the minimum value for row must be 5 to allow for the Y – 5 in lines 3020 and 3030. And since lines 3050 and 3060 add 5 to the value of Y, we make the maximum limit for row 90 instead of 95.

Now RUN the program and place the figure at different places on the screen by INPUTing values for X and Y.

SOUND WITH FIGURE

Let's add a subroutine that introduces some sound each time the figure appears. We'll set it up so that the lower the figure appears on the screen, the lower the sound. Since the higher row numbers correspond to lower screen positions and higher note values correspond to lower notes, we can accomplish this by making the note value a function of Y. While we're at it, let's have the value for hue (H) also affect the note value. This is done in line 5020 of the following subroutine:

```
5000 REM ** SOUND OF STAR SHIP
5010 FOR CYCLE=1 TO 5
5020 SOUND 0,Y/2+H,12,10
5030 NEXT CYCLE
5050 RETURN
```

We've used a value of 12 for the tone parameter here to get a different effect.

Now add a GOSUB statement at line 3080 to call this routine. Finally, add these lines to briefly sustain the last note played and then turn off the sound before the figure disappears.

```
3080 GOSUB 5010
350 FOR P=1 TO 100
360 NEXT P
370 REM ** TURN OFF VOICE 0
380 SOUND 0,0,0,0
```

The complete listing should now be:

```
Ø REM *** MOVING STAR SHIP

1Ø PRINT "ENTER Ø – 139 FOR COLUMN"
2Ø INPUT X
3Ø PRINT
5Ø PRINT "ENTER 5 – 9Ø FOR ROW"
6Ø INPUT Y
7Ø PRINT

1ØØ REM ** SETUP FOR GRAPHICS
11Ø GRAPHICS 23
12Ø COLOR 1

2ØØ REM ** CHANGES HUES
21Ø FOR H=Ø TO 15
22Ø SETCOLOR Ø,H,12
26Ø GOSUB 3Ø1Ø
29Ø NEXT H

35Ø FOR P=1 TO 1ØØ

36Ø NEXT P
37Ø REM ** TURN OFF VOICE Ø
38Ø SOUND Ø,Ø,Ø,Ø

5ØØ REM ** STARTS LOOP AGAIN
51Ø GOTO 1Ø

3ØØØ REM ** DRAW STAR SHIP
3Ø1Ø PLOT X,Y
3Ø2Ø DRAWTO X+5,Y-5
3Ø3Ø DRAWTO X+15,Y-5
3Ø4Ø DRAWTO X+2Ø,Y
3Ø5Ø DRAWTO X+15,Y+5
3Ø6Ø DRAWTO X+5,Y+5
3Ø7Ø DRAWTO X,Y
3Ø8Ø GOSUB 5Ø1Ø
4Ø9Ø RETURN

5ØØØ REM ** SOUND OF STAR SHIP
5Ø1Ø N=Y+H
5Ø2Ø FOR CYCLE=1 TO 5
5Ø3Ø SOUND Ø,N,12,1Ø
5Ø4Ø NEXT CYCLE
5Ø5Ø RETURN
```

RUN the program to hear how the sound works with the different positions of the figure.

Each time through the hue loop in lines 210 through 290, the GOSUB statement at line 260 calls the subroutine to draw the figure. Line 5080 of that routine calls the sound routine (nested subroutines). *Note* gets a value of Y that you have entered, plus the value for H that the hue loop has reached. For example, if you've entered a value of 40 for Y, then N will be 40 + 0 = 40 the first time through the loop and 40 + 1 = 41 the next time, and so on up to 40 + 15 = 55.

After each of the hues has been registered and each of the notes played, we return to lines 350 through 380, which very briefly sustain the note and then turn off the sound. And finally line 510 starts us over again.

IDEAS FOR EXPLORATION

In the next section we will continue to build upon this program, so we suggest that you save it if you have an ATARI 410 Program Record or 810 Disk Drive.

Before going on, try some variations of your own on the program. Here are a few suggestions:

1. Write your own sound routine for the Star Ship.
2. Try graphics mode 7 instead of 23.
3. Try some different values for COLOR in line 120 and for the color register (the first parameter) of the SETCOLOR command in line 130.

For a challenge:

Use FOR-NEXT loops instead of INPUT statements to move the figure around. HINT: For best results, these loops should begin before line 210 and end after line 380. Don't forget to remove the INPUT statements if you try this experiment.

Make sure you have this listing before going on to the next section:

```
Ø REM *** MOVING STAR SHIP
1Ø PRINT "ENTER Ø – 139 FOR COLUMN"
2Ø INPUT X
3Ø PRINT
5Ø PRINT "ENTER 5 – 9Ø FOR ROW"
6Ø INPUT Y
7Ø PRINT

1ØØ REM ** SETUP FOR GRAPHICS
11Ø GRAPHICS 23
12Ø COLOR 1

2ØØ REM ** CHANGES HUES
21Ø FOR H=Ø TO 15
22Ø SETCOLOR Ø,H,12
26Ø GOSUB 3Ø1Ø
29Ø NEXT H

35Ø FOR P=1 TO 1ØØ

36Ø NEXT P
37Ø REM ** TURN OFF VOICE Ø
38Ø SOUND Ø,Ø,Ø,Ø

5ØØ REM ** STARTS LOOP AGAIN
51Ø GOTO 1Ø

3ØØØ REM ** DRAW STAR SHIP
3Ø1Ø PLOT X,Y
3Ø2Ø DRAWTO X+5,Y–5
3Ø3Ø DRAWTO X+15,Y–5
3Ø4Ø DRAWTO X+2Ø,Y
3Ø5Ø DRAWTO X+15,Y+5
3Ø6Ø DRAWTO X+5,Y+5
3Ø7Ø DRAWTO X,Y
3Ø8Ø GOSUB 5Ø1Ø
4Ø9Ø RETURN

5ØØØ REM ** SOUND OF STAR SHIP
5Ø1Ø N=Y+H
5Ø2Ø FOR CYCLE=1 TO 5
5Ø3Ø SOUND Ø,N,12,1Ø
5Ø4Ø NEXT CYCLE
5Ø5Ø RETURN
```

IF-THEN DECISIONS

While you were experimenting with this program, you may have occasionally slipped and entered a value that was too small or too large for X or Y, thus getting an ERROR message and having to start again.

A programming tool that can be used to catch these mistakes without crashing the program is the IF-THEN statement. Essentially, what this statement says is:

IF certain conditions are met, THEN do such and such.

or:

IF certain conditions are not met, ignore the THEN part of the statement and go on to the next line.

For example, suppose in the program we've been using to move the figure on the screen, we want the machine to reprint the instructions in line 1Ø if a value greater than 139 is entered. We can do this with a line like this:

```
4Ø IF X > 139 THEN 1Ø
```

Symbol for "is greater than"

Add this line and RUN the program. Then try entering a value greater than 139 a few times to get the idea. Instead of giving you an ERROR message this time, the machine just prints:

```
ENTER Ø – 139 FOR COLUMN
```

over again. This will happen as many times as you enter incorrect values.

When the conditions of the IF part of the statement are not met—that is, when X is not greater than 139—the THEN part of the statement is ignored and the next line of the program is executed. Have a look at the line again with arrows indicating the different directions the program might take.

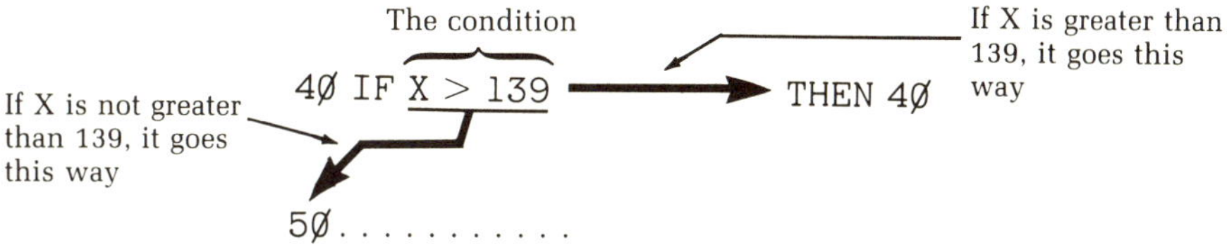

Now let's add a few more lines to account for incorrect values for Y being entered:

```
7Ø IF Y < 5 THEN 5Ø
8Ø If Y > 9Ø THEN 5Ø
```

Less than

Line 7Ø says, IF Y is less than 5, THEN execute line 5Ø again.

Line 8Ø says, IF Y is greater than 9Ø, THEN execute line 5Ø again.

Here's a complete listing of the program including IF-THEN statements to reprint the instructions if an incorrect value for X or Y is entered:

```
Ø REM *** MOVING STAR SHIP

1Ø PRINT "ENTER Ø - 139 FOR COLUMN"
2Ø INPUT X
3Ø PRINT
4Ø IF X>139 THEN 1Ø
5Ø PRINT "ENTER 5 - 9Ø"
6Ø INPUT Y
7Ø IF Y<5 THEN 5Ø
8Ø IF Y>9Ø THEN 5Ø

1ØØ REM ** SETUP FOR GRAPHICS
11Ø GRAPHICS 23
12Ø COLOR 1

2ØØ REM ** CHANGES HUES
21Ø FOR H=Ø TO 15
22Ø SETCOLOR Ø,H,12
26Ø GOSUB 3Ø1Ø
29Ø NEXT H

35Ø FOR P=1 TO 1ØØ
36Ø NEXT P

37Ø REM ** TURN OFF VOICE Ø
38Ø SOUND Ø,Ø,Ø,Ø

5ØØ REM ** STARTS LOOP AGAIN
51Ø GOTO 1Ø

3ØØØ REM ** DRAW STAR SHIP
3Ø1Ø PLOT X,Y
3Ø2Ø DRAWTO X+5,Y-5
3Ø3Ø DRAWTO X+15,Y-5
3Ø4Ø DRAWTO X+2Ø,Y
3Ø5Ø DRAWTO X+15,Y+5
3Ø6Ø DRAWTO X+5,Y+5
3Ø7Ø DRAWTO X,Y
3Ø8Ø GOSUB 5Ø1Ø
4Ø9Ø RETURN

5ØØØ REM ** SOUND OF STAR SHIP
5Ø1Ø FOR CYCLE=1 TO 5
5Ø2Ø SOUND Ø,Y+H,12,1Ø
5Ø3Ø NEXT CYCLE
5Ø5Ø RETURN
```

Rather than reprint the instructions, we can default to 139 any time a value greater than 139 is entered for X by making line 4Ø:

```
4Ø IF X > 139 THEN X=139
```

With these conditions, any time you ENTER a value greater than 139 for X, it will plot the starting point for the figure in column 139. In the same way, lines 8Ø and 9Ø can be changed to:

```
7Ø IF Y < 5 THEN Y=5
8Ø IF Y > 9Ø THEN Y=9Ø
```

Add these lines, RUN the program, and try some values greater than 139 for column and less than 5 or greater than 9Ø for row. This time, when you ENTER an incorrect value for column or row the machine will still draw the figure.

See if you can use this method to limit the area in which the figure is drawn to a specific area of the screen, for example, the left side or the bottom half.

IF-THEN statements can be used to make a number of different kinds of comparisons. We've looked at comparisons based on whether one variable is greater than the other and comparisons based on whether one variable is less than the other. The following chart shows some other comparisons that can be made:

Symbol	*Meaning*
<	less than
>	greater than
=	equal to
<>	not equal to
>=	greater than or equal to
<=	less than or equal to

We'll see more ways to use IF-THEN decisions in the next few chapters.

HIGH-RESOLUTION GRAPHICS MODE

The ATARI Computer has a high-resolution graphics mode that enables you to plot much smaller points and therefore draw much finer lines. This is graphics mode 8, with the text window, or 24, without the text window. Although it is possible to draw without it, you need the SETCOLOR command to introduce color in mode 8 or 24. That's why we've waited until you've learned about the SETCOLOR command before discussing the high-resolution mode.

The number of columns and rows available in graphics modes 8 and 24 are:

	Columns	Rows
Graphics 8	(Ø – 319)	(Ø – 159)
Graphics 24	(Ø – 319)	(Ø – 191)

The "Moving Star Ship" program you've been working with so far will serve as a good starting place to explore high-resolution graphics in ATARI BASIC. Start by changing line 11Ø to:

```
11Ø GRAPHICS 24
```

The significant variable in the SETCOLOR command for this mode will be the color register. Values of 2 and 4 affect the color. Make the color register 4 in the SETCOLOR command in line 22Ø:

```
22Ø SETCOLOR 4,H,12
```

The PRINT statements and IF-THEN statements in the beginning of the program also need to be changed to allow for the larger number of columns and rows available in this graphics mode. Make lines 1Ø through 8Ø:

```
1Ø PRINT "ENTER Ø – 299 FOR COLUMN"
2Ø INPUT X
3Ø PRINT
4Ø IF X/ > 299 THEN 1Ø

5Ø PRINT "ENTER 5 – 186 FOR ROW"
6Ø INPUT Y
7Ø IF Y<5 THEN 5Ø
8Ø IF Y>186 THEN 5Ø
```

The complete program listing should now be:

```
Ø REM *** MOVING STAR SHIP
1 REM *** HIGH RESOLUTION GRAPHICS

1Ø PRINT "ENTER Ø - 299 FOR COLUMN"
2Ø INPUT X
3Ø PRINT
4Ø IF X>299 THEN 1Ø

5Ø PRINT "ENTER 5 - 186 FOR ROW"
6Ø INPUT Y
7Ø IF Y<5 THEN 5Ø
8Ø IF Y>186 THEN 5Ø

1ØØ REM ** SETUP FOR GRAPHICS
11Ø GRAPHICS 24
12Ø COLOR 1

2ØØ REM ** CHANGES HUES
21Ø FOR H=Ø TO 15
22Ø SETCOLOR 4,H,12
26Ø GOSUB 3Ø1Ø
29Ø NEXT H

35Ø FOR P=1 TO 1ØØ
36Ø NEXT P

37Ø REM ** TURN OFF VOICE Ø
38Ø SOUND Ø,Ø,Ø,Ø

5ØØ REM ** STARTS LOOP AGAIN
51Ø GOTO 1Ø

3ØØØ REM ** DRAW STAR SHIP
3Ø1Ø PLOT X,Y
3Ø2Ø DRAWTO X+5,Y-5
3Ø3Ø DRAWTO X+15,Y-5
3Ø4Ø DRAWTO X+2Ø,Y
3Ø5Ø DRAWTO X+15,Y+5
3Ø6Ø DRAWTO X+5,Y+5
3Ø7Ø DRAWTO X,Y
3Ø8Ø GOSUB 5Ø1Ø
4Ø9Ø RETURN

5ØØØ REM ** SOUND OF STAR SHIP
5Ø1Ø FOR CYCLE=1 TO 5
5Ø2Ø SOUND Ø,Y+H,12,1Ø
5Ø3Ø NEXT CYCLE
5Ø5Ø RETURN
```

RUN it and see what happens when you ENTER values for X and Y.

Instead of the hue of the figure or the background screen changing, the border of the screen changes as the hue loop is executed. In graphics mode 24, the color of the border of the screen is changed when color register is 4 in the SETCOLOR command.

Also, the figure is now smaller and drawn with much smaller lines.

What happens when you change the color register to 2 in the SETCOLOR command in line 22Ø?

Here's a trick you may have already discovered in your explorations of the other graphics modes with text windows that has an interesting effect in graphics mode 8.

Although the chart above states that you have fewer rows in which to plot and draw when using the text window, the machine will actually still draw in the rows at the bottom of the screen, but you won't see it because it is covered by the text window. Or to say it a little more logically, you won't get an ERROR message if you plot and draw in the text window area; it just won't show up on the screen. To see what we mean, RUN the "Moving Star Ship" program in graphics mode 8 and ENTER values of 25Ø for column and 16Ø for row. You'll get this on the screen:

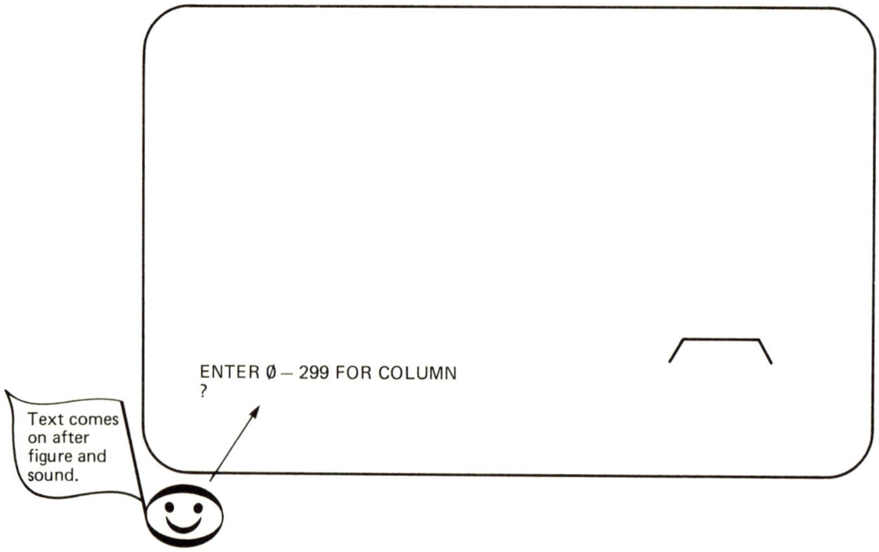

In graphics mode 8, the text window isn't defined by a different color as it is in graphics modes 3 through 7, but it's still there for text to be printed. It also provides an easy way to have the figure cut off at the bottom as it does above. Now INPUT 250 for column and 157 for row. This time you get:

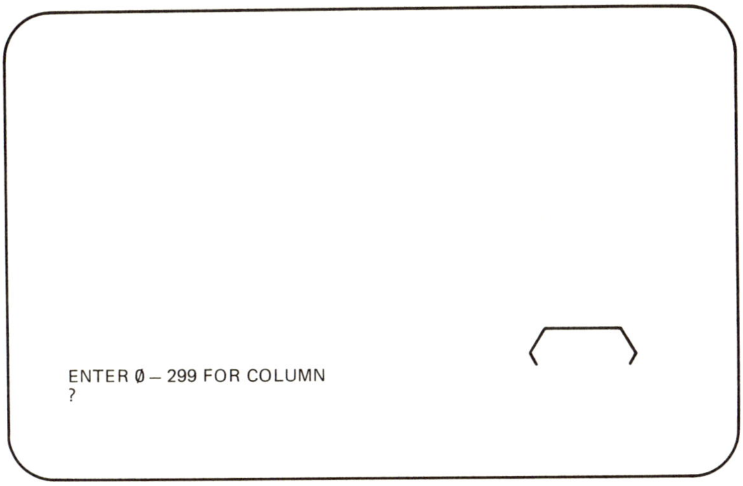

Finally, INPUT 250 for column and 154 for row and the entire figure shows up again:

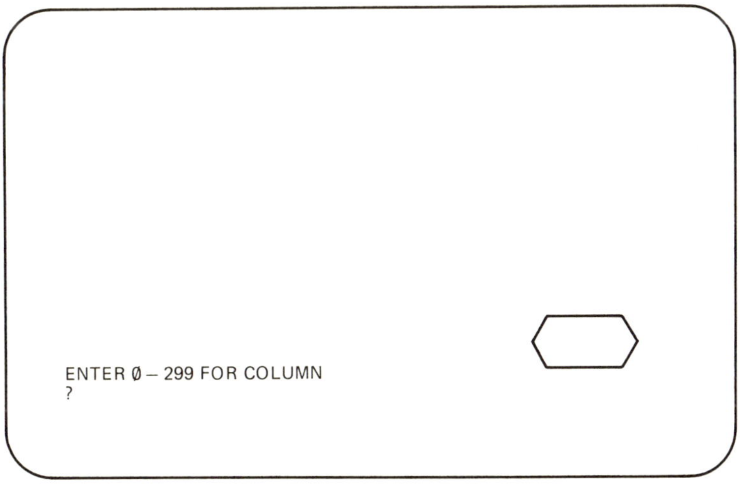

Play around with a few more values for row near 154. You might find this useful in making a figure appear to "rise up out of" the text window area.

Can you think of a way to do this using a FOR-NEXT loop to enter values for X and Y? HINT: The FOR statement for the Y should start at about 170 and use the STEP–1 function. The loops for both X and Y should begin after line 120 and before line 130, and they should end somewhere after line 380.

In this chapter you have built the skeleton of one program and then made several variations in that program to explore different parameters of the SETCOLOR command and to learn a new graphics mode.

You've gained quite a bit of experience in the art of programming by practicing the process of deleting lines, adding others, and moving routines from one place to another. As with anything new, this process may be difficult at first, but as you continue to do it, you'll get better at it.

Self-Test

1. Which parameter is affected by the number 8 in the following command?

```
SETCOLOR 2,8,10
```

2. What value for CR (color register) will enable you to change the color of the background screen below?

```
110 GRAPHICS 19
120 COLOR 1
130 SETCOLOR CR,8,6,
```

3. What does the third parameter of the SETCOLOR command affect?
4. What's wrong with this command?

```
220 SETCOLOR 4,6,5
```

5. The following program draws a square. How might you change it to let the user move the square to different places using INPUT statements?

```
110 GRAPHICS 7
120 COLOR 1
130 SETCOLOR 1,6,10
210 PLOT 10,10
220 DRAWTO 20,10
230 DRAWTO 20,20
240 DRAWTO 10,20
250 DRAWTO 10,10
```

6. What do you think will happen if the machine sees a value greater than 139 in the following line?

```
40 IF X > 139 THEN PRINT "NUMBER TOO BIG"
```

7. What symbol do you think should go after the letter X in line 100 below?

```
100 IF X      2001 THEN 300
.
.
300 PRINT "THE YEAR YOU HAVE CHOSEN IS IN THE FUTURE"
```

8. What is the highest resolution mode in ATARI BASIC?

Answers

1. Hue
2. 4
3. The color luminance, which is the brightness of the color
4. Color luminance should have even numbered values from 0 through 14. The SETCOLOR command shown here has an odd number for color luminance.
5. Something like this:

```
110 GRAPHICS 7
120 COLOR 1
130 SETCOLOR 1,6,10
150 INPUT X
160 INPUT Y
210 PLOT X,Y
220 DRAWTO X+10,Y
230 DRAWTO X+10,Y+10
240 DRAWTO X,Y+10
250 DRAWTO X,Y
260 GOTO 150
```

In this program, the INPUT statements occur after line 130, which will leave the squares on the screen. Otherwise it would draw it so fast that you probably wouldn't see it, and then put the question mark back on the screen.

6. It will print:

```
NUMBER TOO BIG
```

on the screen.

7. The greater than symbol (>)
8. With text window, 8
   Without text window, 24

Challenges

1. In the "Moving Star Ship" program from this chapter, move the INPUT statements to somewhere after line 12Ø and before line 21Ø so that the figures can stay on the screen. Where does the GOTO statement at line 51Ø need to send you now?
2. If you succeed with the first challenge, try making the square routine from Question 5 a subroutine and add some more INPUT statements so you can move the star ship and the square around on the screen.

CHAPTER EIGHT

Chance Music and Graphics

In the preceding chapters, you've used a number of techniques to specify the value of variables in SOUND and GRAPHICS statements.

You may have used a constant value for a particular parameter or entered different values with INPUT statements or FOR-NEXT loops. In each case, however, you have determined a specific value or set of values for a given parameter.

In this chapter you will learn to have the computer generate *random numbers* that can be used in your sound and graphics programs, thus introducing an element of surprise essential to any creative work.

RANDOM NUMBERS

If you've ever been to a raffle where they put 100 tickets numbered from 1 to 100 in a box and someone reaches in the box to pull out the ticket with the winning number, then you've witnessed the selection of a *random number* between 1 and 100.

To generate a random number in ATARI BASIC, use the RND function. To see how it works, ENTER and RUN the following program:

```
0 REM *** PRINT RANDOM NUMBERS
10 PRINT RND(1)
20 FOR P=1 TO 200
30 NEXT P
40 GOTO 10
```

Pretty soon the screen looks something like this:

The numbers you get on the screen won't be the same as the ones here, because they are random (i.e., they are different every time).

Notice that each number has a zero followed by a decimal point and lots of other numbers. This is because it is choosing and printing random numbers between zero and one.

Now change line 1Ø to:

```
1Ø PRINT 1Ø*RND(1)
```

ATARI BASIC's multiplication sign

This time you'll get something like:

RANDOM INTEGERS

For most experiments you'll want to do, you won't need numbers with all that information after the decimal point. You'll only need "whole numbers," or integers like 8, 42, or 256.

To have the computer select random integers change line 1Ø to:

```
1Ø PRINT INT (1Ø*RND(1))
```

Now when you run it, you'll get something like:

```
8
7
3
4
4
9
5
3
6
9
1
4
8
5
2
```

Notice the highest number you ever get is 9. That is because 1Ø *RND(1) tells the computer to pick one of 1Ø random integers from Ø to 9.

If you want to pick from 1 to 1Ø, change line 1Ø to:

```
1Ø PRINT INT(1Ø*RND(1)+1)
```

You can also say:

```
1Ø PRINT INT(1ØØ*(1)+1)
```

for a random integer between 1 and 1ØØ. Or:

```
1Ø PRINT INT(1ØØ*RND(1)+1Ø1)
```

This will generate a random integer between 1ØØ and 2ØØ.

Suppose you want to generate random integers that are only intervals of 10. Here's how you can do it:

```
10 PRINT INT(10*RND(1)+1) * 10
```

Outside of parenthesis

The multiplication by 10 must occur outside the parenthesis here.

As you can see, the RND function can be used in various ways to generate different sets of random numbers or random integers. We suggest you explore this concept a bit more using the PRINT statement to get a thorough understanding of the things you can do with this function.

For example:

Generate random integers between 1 and 500.
Generate random integers between 50 and 60.
Generate random integers in multiples of 25 between 0 and 250.

RANDOM NOTES

You can use random integers just as you would other variables. For example, you might say:

```
0 REM *** RANDOM NOTES
210 SOUND 0,INT(256*RND(1)),10,10
220 FOR P=1 TO 50
230 NEXT P
240 GOTO 210
```

ENTER and RUN this program to hear a note randomly selected and played, then another note, and so on.

The same thing can be accomplished like this:

```
0 REM *** RANDOM NOTES
40 REM *** EACH VOICE WILL GET A NOTE
50 FOR V=0 TO 3

100 REM ** PICKS VALUE FOR N
110 N=INT(256*RND(1))

200 REM ** PLAYS THE NOTE
210 SOUND 0, N, 10, 10
220 FOR P=1 TO 50
230 NEXT P

300 REM ** PICKS ANOTHER NOTE
310 GOTO 110
```

The advantage of this version is that now the value N can be used in other ways. For example, here's a program that continually enters different random note values in each of the four voices:

```
Ø REM *** RANDOM NOTES

4Ø REM *** EACH VOICE WILL GET A NOTE
5Ø FOR V=Ø TO 3

1ØØ REM ** PICKS VALUE FOR N
11Ø N=INT(256*RND(1))

2ØØ REM ** PLAYS THE NOTE
21Ø SOUND V,N,1Ø,1Ø
22Ø FOR P=1 TO 5Ø
23Ø NEXT P

24Ø REM ** ANOTHER VOICE ANOTHER NOTE
25Ø NEXT V
55Ø GOTO 5Ø
```

ENTER and RUN the program to hear what it sounds like before we describe it.

The first time through the FOR-NEXT loop for voice in lines 5Ø through 25Ø, voice Ø is given a random value for note. This voice continues to play that note until the remaining three voices have each been given a random note value of their own and then played. The second time through the loop, voice 1 is given a random note value, which it plays.

When all four voices have been played, line 55Ø starts it over again and voice Ø gets a new note. Each voice continues to play its note while the other three voices are being assigned note values. Thus any given voice gets a new note only every fourth time through the cycle. This is what creates the kind of ongoing but ever-changing, chord-like sound you hear.

THE RND FUNCTION IN GRAPHICS

Now let's add some random graphics to the program. First add these lines:

```
1Ø GRAPHICS 23
2Ø COLOR 1
```

and:

```
13Ø SETCOLOR 4,8,1Ø
```

We're putting the SETCOLOR command within the voice loop (lines 50 through 250) so you will be able to do an experiment with it a little later. For the moment add these lines:

```
150 REM *** LINE DESIGN
160 X=INT(160*RND(1))
170 Y=INT(96*RND(1))
180 PLOT X,Y
190 DRAWTO 75,40
```

The complete program listing should now be:

```
0 REM *** RANDOM NOTES
10 GRAPHICS 23
20 COLOR 1

40 REM *** EACH VOICE WILL GET A NOTE
50 FOR V=0 TO 3

100 REM ** PICKS VALUE FOR N
110 N=INT(256*RND(1))

130 SETCOLOR 4,8,10

150 REM *** LINE DESIGN
160 X=INT(160*RND(1))
170 Y=INT(96*RND(1))
180 PLOT X,Y
190 DRAWTO 75, 40

200 REM ** PLAYS THE NOTE
210 SOUND V,N,10,10
220 FOR P=1 TO 50
230 NEXT P

240 REM ** ANOTHER VOICE ANOTER NOTE
250 NEXT V
550 GOTO 50
```

Rather than us trying to describe what happens, RUN the program to see for yourself.

Lines 160 through 180 plot a point in a random column and row. Line 190 then draws a line from that point to a fixed point near the center of the screen. If you let it RUN for a while, the pattern fills out quite a bit.

Some Ideas for Experimentation

Make the value for hue in the SETCOLOR command in line 130 H instead of 8 and then at line 120 generate a random value for H. Remember hue has sixteen possible values.

In line 220 change the number 50 to some variable like DUR for "duration" of the note and then add a RND function at line 215 to vary the length of note played.

Change the loudness parameter in the sound statement in line 210 to L and add a decay loop in lines 205 and 235. But in order to keep all four voices going, decay only from 15 to 3.

After you've tried these changes on your own, have a look at how we've done it:

```
0 REM *** RANDOM NOTES
10 GRAPHICS 23
20 COLOR 1

40 REM *** EACH VOICE WILL GET A NOTE
50 FOR V=0 TO 3

100 REM ** PICKS VALUE FOR N
110 N=INT(256*RND(1))
120 H=INT(16*RND(1)+1)

130 SETCOLOR 4,H,10

150 REM *** LINE DESIGN
160 X=INT(160*RND(1))
170 Y=INT(96*RND(1))
180 PLOT X,Y
190 DRAWTO 75,40

200 REM ** PLAYS THE NOTE
205 FOR L=15 TO 3 STEP -3
210 SOUND V,N,10,L
215 DUR=INT(10*RND(1))
220 FOR P=1 TO DUR
230 NEXT P
235 NEXT L

240 REM ** ANOTHER VOICE ANOTHER NOTE
250 NEXT V
550 GOTO 50
```

In the next section we'll build a new program, but we suggest you have this one on your ATARI 410 Program Recorder or ATARI 810 Disk Drive system.

RANDOM ELEMENTS WITHIN FORM

The use of random elements in an artistic program raises one of the most misunderstood concepts in the creative process. That is the concept of improvisation or free form. It is often thought that improvisation means "no form." On the contrary, a truly well-crafted improvisation is one that makes use of a deeper understanding of form without obviously manifesting structure. This is truly the essence of art.

We won't get into the question of whether or not a computer can improvise, but the program below is an example of how you can use the RND function to create a piece with slight variations in form each time it runs.

The program draws a mountain range that always consists of twelve mountains. The peaks of the mountains, however, are randomly placed, and the base points from which the sides are drawn are also randomly selected. To get started, ENTER and RUN this initial program:

```
Ø REM *** MOUNTAIN RANGE
1Ø GRAPHICS 24
2Ø COLOR 1
3Ø SETCOLOR 2,8,4

4Ø REM *** THE TWELVE HILLS
5Ø FOR MOUNTAIN=1 TO 12
1ØØ REM *** TOP OF THE MOUNTAIN
11Ø A=INT(32Ø*RND(1))
12Ø B=INT(7Ø*RND(1)+1Ø)

2ØØ REM *** TWELVE SIDES PER HILL
21Ø FOR SIDE=1 TO 12
25Ø REM *** SELECTS BASE POINT
26Ø X=INT(32Ø*RND(1))
27Ø Y=INT(4Ø*RND(1)+1ØØ)

3ØØ REM *** DRAWS FROM BASE TO TOP
31Ø PLOT X,Y
32Ø DRAWTO A,B
499 REM
51Ø NEXT SIDE

9ØØ REM *** DRAWS ANOTHER MOUNTAIN
91Ø NEXT MOUNTAIN
99Ø GOTO 99Ø
```

After setting up the initial graphics mode and colors in lines 1Ø through 3Ø, the FOR-NEXT loop for "Mountain" establishes a cycle in which twelve mountains are drawn. All other routines will be nested within this larger loop.

Lines 110 and 120 randomly select values for the columns and row (A for column and B for row) in which a given mountain peak is to be plotted. The mountain peak is actually determined a bit later by line 320. Line 110 chooses from any of the 320 columns available, but line 120 limits the location of the mountain peaks to the upper part of the screen. The first part of the RND function in that line picks an integer from 0 to 69, and then the second part of the expression adds 10 to give a value between 9 and 79 for the row.

The FOR-NEXT loop in lines 210 through 510 randomly plots points from which twelve lines are drawn to the peak of each mountain. Again line 260 allows these base points to occur in any column, but line 270 limits the row in which a base point is plotted to those from 39 through 139, an area towards the bottom of the screen.

As the FOR-NEXT loop for "side" goes through its twelve cycles, twelve randomly selected base points are plotted at line 310. Line 320 draws a line from each of these points to the mountain's peak, selected in lines 110 and 120. It is important that the mountain peak (point A,B) is selected before the beginning of the FOR-NEXT loop for the sides. This is necessary to have one point to which each of the sides is drawn (i.e., the peak point A,B).

Finally, when this cycle is completed and one mountain with its twelve sides is drawn, line 910 goes back for the "next mountain" beginning at line 50. This larger cycle also occurs twelve times to draw a total of twelve mountains with twelve sides.

Run this program several more times to see how it draws a slightly different mountain range each time.

As you develop your programming skills and strive for more and more sophisticated programs, you must be aware of the time required for the machine to make certain calculations and perform certain functions. To get a sense of this, we will add a sequence of notes to the program after each mountain is drawn and then have you see what happens when you move this sequence to within the loop to draw the sides. Begin by making the additions to the program shown below:

```
0 REM *** MOUNTAIN RANGE
10 GRAPHICS 24
20 COLOR 1
30 SETCOLOR 0,10,10

40 REM *** THE TWELVE HILLS
50 FOR MOUNTAIN=1 TO 12

100 REM *** TOP OF THE MOUNTAIN
110 A=INT(320*RND(1))
120 B=INT(70*RND(1)+10)

200 REM *** TWELVE SIDES PER HILL
210 FOR SIDE=1 TO 12
250 REM *** SELECTS BASE POINT
260 X=INT(320*RND(1))
270 Y=INT(40*RND(1)+100)

300 REM *** DRAWS FROM BASE TO TOP
310 PLOT X,Y
320 DRAWTO A,B

510 NEXT SIDE

600 REM *** NOTE CYCLE
610 FOR NOTE =1 TO 50
620 N=INT(50*RND(1))
630 FOR L=15 TO 0 STEP -5
640 SOUND 0,N,10,L
650 NEXT L
690 NEXT NOTE

900 REM *** DRAWS ANOTHER MOUNTAIN
910 NEXT MOUNTAIN
990 GOTO 990
```

Now when you run the program, you should hear a rapid sequence of notes played after each mountain is drawn. This sequence will be different each time.

This routine randomly selects a note value between 1 and 5 at line 620 and then plays the note with a decay in lines 630 through 650. The FOR-NEXT loop in lines 610 through 690 repeats this cycle a total of 50 times.

Run this program a few more times to fully absorb how it is functioning.

Ideas for Exploration

Change line 620 to randomly select note values from 1 to 100.

Have line 620 randomly select note values between 100 and 150.

In line 110, limit the values for column that are randomly chosen to values between 100 and 200.

Finally, remove lines 610 and 690 and move line 510 down to line 710. This will cause a single note to be played as each line is drawn—a significant change in the program.

Most likely you have had some other ideas you'd like to explore with this program. Please try them and don't be afraid to make some mistakes. It's part of learning to program creatively.

When you've finished your explorations, return to this listing for the program:

```
Ø REM *** MOUTAIN RANGE
1Ø GRAPHICS 24
2Ø COLOR 1
3Ø SETCOLOR Ø,1Ø,1Ø

4Ø REM *** THE TWELVE HILLS
5Ø FOR MOUNTAIN=1 TO 12

1ØØ REM *** TOP OF THE MOUNTAIN
11Ø A=INT(32Ø*RND(1))
12Ø B=INT(7Ø*RND(1)+1Ø)

2ØØ REM *** TWELVE SIDES PER HILL
21Ø FOR SIDE=1 TO 12
25Ø REM *** SELECTS BASE POINT
26Ø X=INT(32Ø*RND(1))
27Ø Y=INT(4Ø*RND(1)+1ØØ)

3ØØ REM *** DRAWS FROM BASE TO TOP
31Ø PLOT X,Y
32Ø DRAWTO A,B

51Ø NEXT SIDE

6ØØ REM *** NOTE CYCLE
61Ø FOR NOTE=1 TO 5Ø
62Ø N=INT(5Ø*RND(1))
63Ø FOR L=15 TO Ø STEP -5
64Ø SOUND Ø,N,1Ø,L
65Ø NEXT L
69Ø NEXT NOTE

9ØØ REM *** DRAWS ANOTHER MOUNTAIN
91Ø NEXT MOUNTAIN
99Ø GOTO 99Ø
```

THE PICTURE FRAME

We can take advantage of the fact that in graphics mode 24 the SETCOLOR command allows us to change the hue of the perimeter of the screen to make an "electric frame" for our picture in this program. This is done by using color register 4 in the SETCOLOR command, which allows changing the hue of the screen perimeter and then creating a FOR-NEXT loop for hue. This can be accomplished with the following program:

```
Ø REM *** MOUNTAIN RANGE
1Ø GRAPHICS 24
2Ø COLOR 1

3Ø SETCOLOR Ø,1Ø,1Ø
4Ø REM *** THE TWELVE HILLS
5Ø FOR MOUNTAIN=1 TO 12

1ØØ REM *** TOP OF THE MOUNTAIN
11Ø A=INT(32Ø*RND(1))
12Ø B=INT(7Ø*RND(1)+1Ø)

2ØØ REM *** TWELVE SIDES PER HILL
21Ø FOR SIDE=1 TO 12
25Ø REM *** SELECTS BASE POINT
26Ø X=INT(32Ø*RND(1))
27Ø Y=INT(4Ø*RND(1)+1ØØ)
3ØØ REM *** DRAWS FROM BASE TO TOP
31Ø PLOT X,Y
32Ø DRAWTO A,B

4ØØ REM *** MODERN PICTURE FRAME
41Ø FOR H=4 TO 9
42Ø SETCOLOR 4,H,4
49Ø NEXT H

51Ø NEXT SIDE

6ØØ REM *** NOTE CYCLE
61Ø FOR NOTE=1 TO 5Ø
62Ø N=INT(5Ø*RND(1))
63Ø FOR L=15 TO Ø STEP -5
64Ø SOUND Ø,N,1Ø,L
65Ø NEXT L
69Ø NEXT NOTE

9ØØ REM *** DRAWS ANOTHER MOUNTAIN
91Ø NEXT MOUNTAIN
99Ø GOTO 99Ø
```

A value of 9 for hue as the loop is finished gives the perimeter of the screen the same hue as the rest of the background. This creates the effect of having the frame occur off and on during the program.

RUN it a few times to fully appreciate the effect.

EXPLOSION SOUNDS

Since the process of a mountain range evolving is really a very stormy one with many volcanic eruptions and such, let's add some explosion sounds to the program. Make the changes in the program as follows:

```
Ø REM *** MOUNTAIN RANGE
1Ø GRAPHICS 24
2Ø COLOR 1
3Ø SETCOLOR Ø,1Ø,1Ø

4Ø REM *** THE TWELVE HILLS
5Ø FOR MOUNTAIN=1 TO 12

1ØØ REM *** TOP OF THE MOUNTAIN
11Ø A=INT(32Ø*RND(1))
12Ø B=INT(7Ø*RND(1)+1Ø)

2ØØ REM *** TWELVE SIDES PER HILL
21Ø FOR SIDE=1 TO 12
25Ø REM *** SELECTS BASE POINT
26Ø X=INT(32Ø*RND(1))
27Ø Y=INT(4Ø*RND(1)+1ØØ)

3ØØ REM *** DRAWS FROM BASE TO TOP
31Ø PLOT X,Y
32Ø DRAWTO A,B,

4ØØ REM *** MODERN PICTURE FRAME
41Ø FOR H=4 TO 9
42Ø SETCOLOR 4,H,4
49Ø NEXT H

51Ø NEXT SIDE

6ØØ REM *** NOTE CYCLE
61Ø FOR NOTE=1 TO 5Ø
62Ø N=INT(5Ø*RND(1))
63Ø FOR L=15 TO Ø STEP -5
64Ø SOUND Ø,N,1Ø,L
65Ø NEXT L
69Ø NEXT NOTE

7ØØ REM *** SOUND TRACK
71Ø EXPL=INT(3*RND(1)+1)
72Ø IF EXPL=1 THEN GOSUB 2Ø1Ø
```

```
900 REM *** DRAWS ANOTHER MOUNTAIN
910 NEXT MOUNTAIN
950 GOSUB 2010
990 GOTO 990

2000 REM *** EXPLOSION SOUND
2010 N=INT(10*RND(1)+1)*10
2020 FOR L=15 TO 0 STEP -1
2030 SOUND 0,N,0,L
2040 SOUND 1,N+1,0,L
2050 SOUND 2,N+2,0,L
2060 SOUND 3,N/2,0,L
2070 FOR P=1 TO 50
2080 NEXT P
2090 NEXT L
3000 RETURN
```

Now RUN the program. Occasionally it should stop after it has drawn a mountain and create an explosion-type sound. If you RUN the program a few times, you'll notice that this explosion occurs at different places in the sequences of mountains being drawn and that the explosion sounds a little different each time.

Line 710 picks a random value between 1 and 3 for "EXPL." The IF-THEN statement in line 720 says if EXPL equals 1, then go down and execute the explosion subroutine at line 2010. If the random value chosen for EXPL is 2 or 3, then it goes on to line 910 with no explosion before it draws the next mountain.

Whenever the "explosion" subroutine is activated, line 2010 randomly selects a value between 1 and 10 and then multiplies this integer by 10 to give N a random value of 10, 20, 30, . . . up to 100.

An explosion sound is actually a very complex wave form often called *white noise* in psycho-acoustics. This can be approximated as we have done here by using a value of 0 for the tone parameter, and playing note values very close to each other with voices 0, 1, and 2 (lines 2030 through 2050) while voice 3 plays a note one octave higher than voice 0 (line 2060). The addition to the decay cycles (lines 2020 through 2090) with the slight pause at each loudness (lines 2070 and 2080) creates the loud percussive beginning with an explosion that decreases in volume.

The purpose of choosing different values for line 2010 is to give each explosion a slightly varied effect. This would naturally occur if you were located in one place and explosions were happening around at different distances and coming from different directions.

Ideas for Exploration

The formula we have used for creating the explosion sound in subroutine 2010 is not an absolute formula. You can make variations of your own to get just the sound you want for an explosion. Here are some ideas.

Change line 2010 to randomly select some other values for N. Remember there are 256 values to choose from.

Put INPUT statement before line 10 of the program and change the tone parameter to a variable so you can experiment with different values for tone in the explosion subroutine. Can you think of a way to INPUT different tone values in different SOUND statements here?

Vary the length of the pause in lines 2070 and 2080.

When you've finished your explorations, make sure you have the listing for the next section.

```
0 REM *** MOUNTAIN RANGE
10 GRAPHICS 24
20 COLOR 1
30 SETCOLOR 0,10,10

40 REM *** THE TWELVE HILLS
50 FOR MOUNTAIN=1 TO 12

100 REM *** TOP OF THE MOUNTAIN
110 A=INT(320*RND(1))
120 B=INT(70*RND(1)+10)

200 REM *** TWELVE SIDES PER HILL
210 FOR SIDE=1 TO 12
250 REM *** SELECTS BASE POINT
260 X=INT(320*RND(1))
270 Y=INT(40*RND(1)+100)

300 REM *** DRAWS FROM BASE TO TOP
310 PLOT X,Y
320 DRAWTO A,B

400 REM *** MODERN PICTURE FRAME
410 FOR H=4 TO 9
420 SETCOLOR 4,H,4
490 NEXT H

510 NEXT SIDE
```

```
600 REM *** NOTE CYCLE
610 FOR NOTE=1 TO 50
620 N=INT(50*RND(1))
630 FOR L=15 TO 0 STEP -5
640 SOUND 0,N,10,L
650 NEXT L
690 NEXT NOTE

700 REM *** SOUND TRACK
710 EXPL=INT(3*RND(1)+1)
720 IF EXPL=1 THEN GOSUB 2010

900 REM *** DRAWS ANOTHER MOUNTAIN
910 NEXT MOUNTAIN
950 GOSUB 2010
990 GOTO 990

2000 REM ** EXPLOSION SOUND
2010 N=INT(10*RND(1)+1)*10
2020 FOR L=15 TO 0 STEP -1
2030 SOUND 0,N,0,L
2040 SOUND 1,N+1,0,L
2050 SOUND 2,N+2,0,L
2060 SOUND 3,N/2,0,L
2070 FOR P=1 TO 50
2080 NEXT P
2090 NEXT L
3000 RETURN
```

For a final addition to our program let's make use of the technique we learned in the last chapter to move the same figure from one place to another on the screen. We'll have a UFO fly across the bottom of the screen.

First delete line 99Ø and then add the following lines:

```
1ØØØ REM *** UFO
1Ø1Ø FOR A=1Ø TO 3ØØ STEP 3
1Ø2Ø B=17Ø
1Ø3Ø COLOR 1
1Ø4Ø GOSUB 4Ø1Ø
1Ø5Ø COLOR Ø
1Ø6Ø GOSUB 4Ø1Ø
1Ø7Ø SOUND Ø,INT(25*RND(1)),1Ø,1Ø
1Ø8Ø NEXT A
1Ø9Ø SOUND Ø,Ø,Ø,Ø
1Ø95 GOTO 1Ø95
```

The UFO:

```
2ØØØ REM ** EXPLOSION SOUND
2Ø1Ø N=INT(1Ø*RND(1)+1)*1Ø
2Ø2Ø FOR L=15 TO Ø STEP -1
2Ø3Ø SOUND Ø,N,Ø,L
2Ø4Ø SOUND 1,N+1,Ø,L
2Ø5Ø SOUND 2,N+2,Ø,L
2Ø6Ø SOUND 3,N/2,Ø,L
2Ø7Ø FOR P=1 TO 5Ø
2Ø8Ø NEXT P
2Ø9Ø NEXT L
3ØØØ RETURN
```

```
4ØØØ REM *** DRAWS UFO
4Ø1Ø SETCOLOR 4,INT(15*RND(1)),1Ø
4Ø2Ø PLOT A,B
4Ø3Ø DRAWTO A+2,B-2
4Ø4Ø DRAWTO A+6,B
4Ø5Ø DRAWTO A+2,B+2
4Ø6Ø DRAWTO A,B
4Ø9Ø RETURN
```

RUN the program with these lines added, and you should see the figure move across the bottom of the screen with a high note played and the perimeter of the screen changing each time the figure appears.

The FOR-NEXT loop in lines 1Ø1Ø establishes plot points for column (A) at 1Ø, 13, 16, etc., across the screen to column 3ØØ. The value for row (B) is constant at row 17Ø.

Lines 1Ø3Ø and 1Ø4Ø enter COLOR 1 and then execute the subroutine to draw the figure. Lines 1Ø5Ø and 1Ø6Ø erase the figure. After the figure has been drawn and erased, a random note is played. Then the cycle begins again. The value of COLOR 1 in line 1Ø3Ø isn't really necessary the first time through the cycle since it has been entered in line 2Ø. However, once the machine has used COLOR Ø at line 1Ø5Ø, it will stay in COLOR Ø until it is given another value for color. So line 1Ø3Ø becomes important after the first time through the cycle.

Line 4Ø1Ø of the "Draws UFO" subroutine is the one that causes the perimeter of the screen to change colors. We've used an RND function to choose one of the sixteen possible values for hue each time the subroutine is executed.

Here's the complete listing of the program:

```
REM *** MOUNTAIN RANGE

1Ø GRAPHICS 24
2Ø COLOR 1
3Ø SETCOLOR Ø,1Ø,1Ø

4Ø REM *** THE TWELVE HILLS
5Ø FOR MOUNTAIN=1 TO 12

1ØØ REM *** TOP OF THE MOUNTAIN
11Ø A=INT(32Ø*RND(1))
12Ø B=INT(7Ø*RND(1)+1Ø)

2ØØ REM *** TWELVE SIDES PER HILL
21Ø FOR SIDE=1 TO 12
25Ø REM *** SELECTS BASE POINT
26Ø X=INT(32Ø*RND(1))
27Ø Y=INT(4Ø*RND(1)+1ØØ)

3ØØ REM *** DRAWS FROM BASE TO TOP
31Ø PLOT X,Y
32Ø DRAWTO A,B

4ØØ REM *** MODERN PICTURE FRAME
41Ø FOR H=4 TO 9
42Ø SETCOLOR 4,H,4
49Ø NEXT H

51Ø NEXT SIDE

6ØØ REM *** NOTE CYCLE
61Ø FOR NOTE=1 TO 5Ø
62Ø N=INT(5Ø*RND(1))
63Ø FOR L=15 TO Ø STEP -5
64Ø SOUND Ø,N,1Ø,L
65Ø NEXT L
69Ø NEXT NOTE
```

```
700 REM *** SOUND TRACK
710 EXPL=INT(3*RND(1)+1)
720 IF EXPL=1 THEN GOSUB 2010

900 REM *** DRAWS ANOTHER MOUNTAIN
910 NEXT MOUNTAIN
950 GOSUB 2010

1000 REM *** UFO
1010 FOR A=10 TO 300 STEP 3
1020 B=170
1030 COLOR 1
1040 GOSUB 4010
1050 COLOR 0
1060 GOSUB 4010
1070 SOUND 0,INT(25*RND(1)),10,10
1080 NEXT A
1090 SOUND 0,0,0,0
1095 GOTO 1095

2000 REM ** EXPLOSION SOUND
2010 N=INT(10*RND(1)+1)*10
2020 FOR L=15 TO 0 STEP -1
2030 SOUND 0,N,0,L
2040 SOUND 1,N+1,0,L
2050 SOUND 2,N+2,0,L
2060 SOUND 3,N/2,0,L
2070 FOR P=1 TO 50
2080 NEXT P
2090 NEXT L
3000 RETURN

4000 REM *** DRAWS UFO
4010 SETCOLOR 4,INT(15*RND(1)),10
4020 PLOT A,B
4030 DRAWTO A+2,B-2
4040 DRAWTO A+6,B
4050 DRAWTO A+2,B+2
4060 DRAWTO A,B
4090 RETURN
```

In this chapter you have learned several ways to use RND functions to create varations in the sound and graphics of a program. Although the two programs in this chapter might be considered "fine art" (that is they have no particular purpose other than to be enjoyed), the techniques can just as easily be used in "functional" programs, such as educational aids or games.

We'll make use of these techniques and others in the coming chapters to create a pitch-matching game.

Heraclitus, the ancient Greek philosopher, was believed to have once said:

> "You can't step in the same river twice."

By this he meant that the river is always changing, and so are you.

When we introduce the RND function into a program we might paraphrase Heraclitus and say:

> "You can't run the same program twice."

The program is always changing, and so are you.

Self-Test

1. What range of numbers will the following program PRINT?

```
10 PRINT 20*RND(1)
20 GOTO 10
```

2. What must be added to line 10 above to PRINT only random integers?
3. What must line 10 of the same program be if you wish to PRINT random integers from 1 through 20?
4. What must line 110 be in this program to randomly generate an even integer from 0 to 14 for tone?

```
100 REM *** RANDOM TONES
110 ____________________
120 SOUND 0,20,T,10
130 FOR P=1 TO 100
140 NEXT P
150 GOTO 110
```

5. Graphics mode 19 has 40 columns (0 through 39) and 24 rows (0 through 23). Add lines 110 and 120 to the following program to randomly choose plot points for column (A) and row (B):

```
10 GRAPHICS 19
20 COLOR 1
30 SETCOLOR 0,8,10
130 PLOT A,B
140 GOTO 10
```

6. Will the notes in this program be high or low notes?

```
100 REM *** FLIGHT OF THE HONEY BEE
110 N=INT(25*RND(1)+225)
120 SOUND 0,N,10,10
130 FOR P=1 TO 5
140 NEXT P
150 GOTO 110
```

7. How would you change line 710 of the final program in this chapter to make it equally likely that the explosion will or will not occur?
8. Change line 1020 of the final program from this chapter so that it picks from all of the 256 possible note values.

Answers

1. From 0 through 19
2. Make line 10:

```
10 PRINT INT(20*RND(1))
```

3. Line 10 becomes:

```
10 PRINT INT(20*RND(1)+1)
```

4. Line 110 should be:

```
110 T = INT(8*RND(1))*2
```

5. Lines 110 and 120 become:

```
110 A = INT(39*RND(1))
120 B = INT(23*RND(1))
```

6. Low notes
7. Make line 710:

```
710 EXPL = INT(2*RND(1) + 1)
```

8. Lines 1070 becomes:

```
1020 SOUND 0, INT(256*RND(1)),10,10
```

Challenges

1. Change line 1Ø2Ø so that the figure stays in the bottom area of the screen but moves up and down instead of going straight across. HINT: You need to randomly select values for rows between about 15Ø and 18Ø.
2. Add some blinking stars to the picture.

CHAPTER NINE

String Variables

As you've been exploring and learning about your ATARI 4ØØ or 8ØØ Computer, you've made frequent use of INPUT statements to enter numeric variables. You've also learned to have the computer compare different numeric values and respond according to conditions you establish with IF-THEN statements.

In this chapter we will look at ways to work with *string variables*. This will allow you to have the computer respond to words and letters as variables also. As you will see a bit later in the chapter, this will be valuable when working with musical notes that are usually defined by letters like C or F#.

STRINGS

Although you may not have seen the term before, you have already worked with *strings* quite a bit in some of the programs you've been using. Often when you've used a PRINT statement, you have actually had the machine print a string. For example:

```
11Ø PRINT "MUSIC IS MORE THAN JUST NOTES"
```

The information between the quotation marks is the string. The quotation marks are *not* part of the string.

Another example of a string would be:

```
11Ø PRINT "C2"
```

In this case the string includes both a letter and a number.

A string may include:

Numerals (Ø,1,2 . . .)
Letters (A,B,C, . . .)
Special characters (–, +, =, # . . .)

Combinations of these are also appropriate as strings. For example, the following are all strings:

C#
C MAJOR 7
F# MINOR
C2

Since the quotation marks are not part of the string, you can't use them in the string. For example, if you try to say:

```
11Ø PRINT "THIS "PRINT STATEMENT" WON'T WORK"
```

you get an ERROR message. So if you are typing in an elaborate string, be sure to avoid using the quotation marks as symbols.

String Variables

In ATARI BASIC the symbol for a *string variable* is a letter of the alphabet followed by a dollar sign ($). You might use something like:

A$
Z$
P$

Before you use a string variable, you must tell the computer how long the string might be. That is, you must reserve a place in the computer's memory to put the string while it is waiting to be used. This is done with a DIMension statement. For example, the following DIM statement tells the computer to make room for a string of up to five characters in length.

```
1Ø DIM A$(5)
```

Dimension — String — Of five characters

To see the string A$ used as a variable, ENTER and RUN the following program:

```
10 DIM A$(5)
110 A$="MUSIC"
120 PRINT A$
130 GOTO 120
```

Pretty soon the screen looks like this:

Line 10 dimensions the string for up to five characters. That is, it reserves space for five characters in the computer's memory.

Line 110 says the string A$ is MUSIC, and then lines 120 and 130 print the string over and over.

A string may be dimensioned for more characters than it will contain, but it cannot be dimensioned for fewer characters. For example,

```
10 DIM A$(10)
```

would work in the program above, but if you entered:

```
10 DIM A$(4)
```

it would print:

```
MUSI
MUSI
MUSI
MUSI
MUSI
MUSI
MUSI
MUSI
MUSI
MUSI
MUSI
MUSI
MUSI
```

Try making line 10:

```
10 DIM A$(2)
```

and RUN the program to see what that does.

The computer will accept only as many characters for a string as you tell it to in the DIM statement. If you type in a longer string, it ignores any characters beyond the number for which it has been dimensioned.

Spaces also count as characters when you dimension a string. The string NEW MUSIC is nine characters long (eight letters and one space).

ENTER and RUN this program to print NEW MUSIC.

```
10 DIM B$(9)
110 B$="NEW MUSIC"
120 PRINT B$
130 GOTO 120
```

Now change line 10 to:

```
10 DIM B$(4)
```

and RUN the program to see what happens.

You may use more than one letter to define a string variable:

```
AZ$
PD$
```

or a letter and a number:

```
A1$
G4$
```

but if you try to use the symbols at the top of the keyboard such as:

```
A%$
A#Z$
```

you'll get an ERROR message. Don't get confused here between the symbol for the string variable and the actual information in the string. For example:

```
1Ø DIM A#B$(1Ø)
2Ø A#B$="MUSIC"
```

will give you an ERROR.
But this works:

```
1Ø DIM A$(1Ø)
2Ø A$="MUSIC #4"
```

ASK FOR MUSIC

You can use strings as variables in many of the same ways that you've been using numerals as variables in other programs. The following program uses the string Z$ with an INPUT statement, an IF-THEN statement, and a PRINT statement:

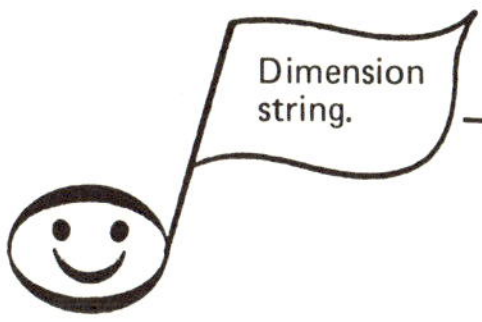

```
Ø REM *** ASK FOR MUSIC

1Ø DIM Z$(1Ø)

1ØØ REM *** INSTRUCTIONS
11Ø PRINT
12Ø PRINT
13Ø PRINT "TO HEAR THE MUSIC"
14Ø PRINT "TYPE THE WORD 'MUSIC'"
15Ø PRINT "AND PRESS RETURN"

2ØØ REM *** ENTER STRING
21Ø INPUT Z$

3ØØ REM *** LOOKS AT STRING
31Ø IF Z$="MUSIC" THEN 51Ø
32Ø IF Z$<> "MUSIC" THEN 41Ø

4ØØ REM *** NO MUSIC
41Ø PRINT
42Ø PRINT "SORRY I DON'T KNOW"
43Ø PRINT "HOW TO PLAY"
44Ø PRINT Z$
49Ø GOTO 11Ø

500 REM ** PLAYS THE MUSIC
51Ø FOR CYCLE=1 TO 5Ø
53Ø N=INT(25*RND(1)+1)*12
54Ø SOUND Ø,N,1Ø,1Ø
55Ø FOR P=1 TO 25
56Ø NEXT P
57Ø NEXT CYCLE
58Ø SOUND Ø,Ø,Ø,Ø
59Ø GOTO 11Ø
```

ENTER and RUN this program. After the instructions appear on the screen, type either the word MUSIC or something else and press RETURN.

Whatever you type is stored as the string Z$ by the INPUT statement at line 210. If you type MUSIC, the IF-THEN statement at line 310 compares the string Z$ to "MUSIC" and then goes to line 510 and plays some music. If, however, you type something else, the INPUT statement at line 210 stores that at Z$. Let's say you type DOG. It stores the string DOG at Z$. In line 310 it sees that DOG is not equal to MUSIC, so it doesn't play any music, but goes to line 320. In line 320 the proper conditions for the IF-THEN statement are met. That is, the string Z$, which is DOG, is not equal to MUSIC, so it goes to line 410. The PRINT statement at line 410 just prints a blank space to separate what follows from any previous text on the screen. It then executes the PRINT statements in line 420 and 430. Then it prints Z$, which in this case is DOG. The result on the screen is:

```
SORRY I DON'T KNOW
HOW TO PLAY
DOG
```

Line 490 goes back to line 110 where it prints two blank spaces and then the instructions again.

Explorations

1. Could Z$ be dimensioned for fewer characters in line 10 and have the program run the same?
2. Add a line at 520 to have the computer PRINT Z$.

Answers

1. Yes, it could be as small as:

```
10 DIM Z$(5)
```

since the string "MUSIC" has only five characters.
2. Line 520 should be:

```
520 PRINT Z$
```

RUN the program like this and see what happens.

TWO STRINGS IN ONE PROGRAM

You can use more than one string in a program, but you must be sure to dimension each string you use. Here's an example of a program that has two strings, A$ and B$:

```
Ø REM *** OLD AND NEW
1 REM *** MUZIO CLEMENTI
2 REM *** HERB MOORE
```

Dimensions each string

```
1Ø DIM A$(1Ø)
2Ø DIM B$(1Ø)
```

```
1ØØ REM *** THE STRINGS
```

Defines the strings

```
11Ø A$="OLD MUSIC"
12Ø B$="NEW MUSIC"
```

```
2ØØ REM *** PICKS OLD OR NEW
21Ø X=INT(2*RND(1)+1)
22Ø IF X=1 THEN 51Ø
23Ø IF X=2 THEN 61Ø

5ØØ REM *** OLD SONG-CLEMENTI
51Ø PRINT
515 PRINT
```

Prints "old music"

```
52Ø PRINT A$
53Ø FOR CYCLE=1 TO 16
```

Reads notes from Clementi theme

```
535 READ N
54Ø SOUND Ø,N,1Ø,1Ø
545 FOR P=1 TO 25
55Ø NEXT P
555 NEXT CYCLE
56Ø DATA 162,121,96,81
565 DATA 91,96,1Ø8,121
57Ø DATA 72,81,91,96
575 DATA 1Ø8,121,128,144
```

Restores notes

```
58Ø RESTORE
59Ø GOTO 21Ø

6ØØ REM *** NEW SONG-HERB + RND
61Ø PRINT
615 PRINT
```

Prints "new music"

```
62Ø PRINT B$
63Ø FOR CYCLE=1 TO 16
```

Randomly selects and plays notes for new music

```
64Ø N=INT(25*RND(1)+1)*12
65Ø SOUND Ø,N,1Ø,1Ø
66Ø FOR P=1 TO 15
67Ø NEXT P
68Ø NEXT CYCLE
```

```
69Ø GOTO 21Ø
```

ENTER and RUN this program and you hear the computer randomly choose between a theme by the Italian composer Muzio Clementi (1752–1832) and some modern sounds. When it plays Clementi, it prints OLD MUSIC on the screen; when it plays the modern theme, it prints NEW MUSIC on the screen.

FANCY PRINTING

Since we've been using graphics modes 3 through 8 so far, you may have wondered about graphics modes 1 and 2. These modes are *text modes* that allow you to print information on the screen with fancy, colorful letters. They will print information in the text window that is just like the text in other graphics modes, but if you want to use big, colorful letters in the graphics display area, you must use a *device number*.

Many of the pieces of equipment associated with your ATARI Computer are called input/output devices (sometimes abbreviated I/O). As the name would imply, they let you INPUT information to the computer and/or OUTPUT information from the computer. The keyboard with which you enter information into the computer's memory is an input device. The ATARI 400 Cassette Recorder and the ATARI 800 Disk Drive system are input/output devices. The TV monitor is also an input/output device.

It is not within the scope of this book to give a detailed description of the ATARI Computer's hardware, but it is valuable to know that each of these devices has a *device number* that must be used in certain operations.

In order to print in the graphics display area in modes 1 or 2, the PRINT statement must take the following form:

```
10 GR. 1
20 COLOR 1
110 PRINT #6;"NEW MUSIC"
```

ENTER and RUN the following program to see what the fancy printing looks like in graphics mode 1:

```
0 REM *** FANCY PRINTING

10 GRAPHICS 1
20 COLOR 1
30 SETCOLOR 0,8,8

100 REM *** TEXT IN GRAPHICS DISPLAY
120 PRINT #6;"MUSIC"

200 REM *** KEEPS IT ON SCREEN
```

You should see something like this appear on the screen:

Now change line 10 to:

```
10 GR. 2
```

and RUN the program.

This time it should print letters of the same height, but twice as wide.

If you think of each letter taking up one plot point, the word MUSIC appears in columns 0 through 4 and in row 1. The number of columns and rows available in graphics modes 1 and 2 is:

Graphics Mode	*Columns*	*Rows*
1	(Ø through 19)	(Ø through 19)
2	(Ø through 19)	(Ø through 9)

To print several lines in graphics modes 1 and 2, you must use the punctuation #6; in each PRINT statement. For example:

```
Ø REM *** FANCY PRINTING

1Ø GRAPHICS 2
2Ø COLOR 1
3Ø SETCOLOR Ø,8,8

1ØØ REM *** TEXT IN GRAPHICS DISPLAY
12Ø PRINT #6;"NEW"
14Ø PRINT #6;"MUSIC"

2ØØ REM *** KEEPS IT ON SCREEN
```

ENTER and RUN this program.

Which columns and rows are being used in the PRINT statements in lines 12Ø and 13Ø?

The string "NEW" appears in columns Ø through 2, row Ø.

The string "MUSIC" appears in columns Ø through 4, row 1.

You can also eliminate the text window in graphics modes 1 and 2 by adding 16 as you did with other modes.

GRAPHICS	1 + 16	or GRAPHICS 17
GRAPHICS	2 + 16	or GRAPHICS 18

Try the program above in graphics modes 17 and 18.

POSITION YOUR PRINTING

In the "Old and New" program from earlier in this chapter, we printed spaces between lines by adding PRINT statements with no strings, as in lines 51Ø and 515. ATARI BASIC also has a command that allows you to place text at different locations on the screen; it is the POSITION command. If you wish to center the strings "NEW" and "MUSIC" on the screen, you can use the POSITION command like this:

```
Ø REM *** FANCY PRINTING

1Ø GRAPHICS 18
2Ø COLOR 1
3Ø SETCOLOR Ø,8,8

1ØØ REM *** TEXT IN GRAPHICS DISPLAY
11Ø POSITION 7,3
12Ø PRINT #6;"NEW"
13Ø POSITION 6,5
14Ø PRINT #6;"MUSIC"

2ØØ REM *** KEEPS IT ON SCREEN
21Ø GOTO 21Ø
```

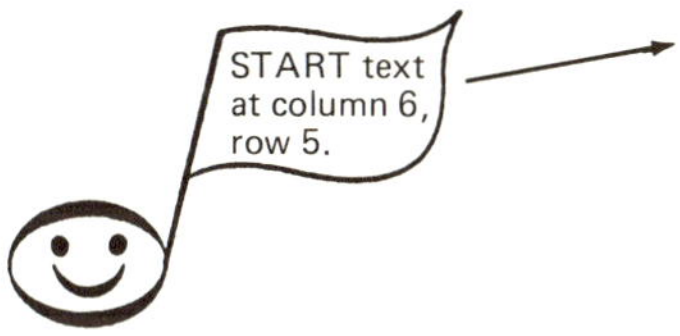

RUN the program and the screen should look like this:

Line 11Ø tells the computer to begin the string "NEW" at column 7 and row 3.

Line 13Ø tells it to begin the string "MUSIC" at column 6 and row 5.

Explorations

See if you can create this on the screen:

BACK TO THE "OLD AND NEW"

Now let's go back to the "Old and New" program we were using earlier in this chapter and instead of printing OLD MUSIC or NEW MUSIC in normal text as it plays the sounds like this:

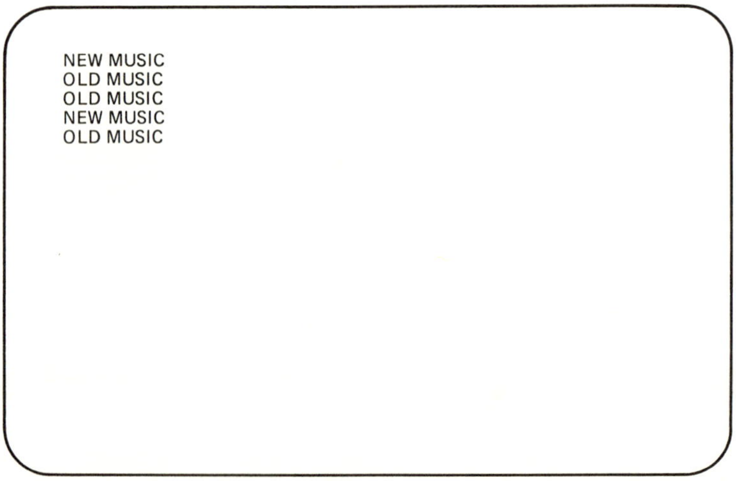

we'll have it print either OLD MUSIC or NEW MUSIC in big letters in the center of the screen like this:

First look at the version of the program that prints in normal text:

```
Ø REM *** OLD AND NEW
1 REM *** MUZIO CLEMENTI
2 REM *** HERB MOORE
1Ø DIM A$(1Ø)
2Ø DIM B$(1Ø)

1ØØ REM *** THE STRINGS
11Ø A$="OLD MUSIC"
12Ø B$="NEW MUSIC"

2ØØ REM *** PICKS OLD OR NEW
21Ø X=INT(2*RND(1)+1)
22Ø IF X=1 THEN 51Ø
23Ø IF X=2 THEN 61Ø

5ØØ REM *** OLD SONG-CLEMENTI
51Ø PRINT
515 PRINT
52Ø PRINT A$
53Ø FOR CYCLE=1 TO 16
535 READ N
54Ø SOUND Ø,N,1Ø,1Ø
545 FOR P=1 TO 25
55Ø NEXT P
555 NEXT CYCLE
56Ø DATA 162,121,96,81
565 DATA 91,96,1Ø8,121
57Ø DATA 72,81,91,96
575 DATA 1Ø8,121,128,144
58Ø RESTORE
59Ø GOTO 21Ø

6ØØ REM *** NEW SONG-HERB + RND
61Ø PRINT
615 PRINT
62Ø PRINT B$
63Ø FOR CYCLE=1 TO 16
64Ø N=INT(25*RND(1)+1)*12
65Ø SOUND Ø,N,1Ø,1Ø
66Ø FOR P=1 TO 15
67Ø NEXT P
68Ø NEXT CYCLE
69Ø GOTO 21Ø
```

Now add the following lines:

```
3Ø GRAPHICS 18
4Ø COLOR 1
6Ø H=INT(16*RND(1))
7Ø SETCOLOR 4,H,4
```

Now replace line 51Ø and change line 52Ø as follows:

```
51Ø POSITION 5,4
52Ø PRINT #6;A$
```

and do the same with lines 61Ø and 62Ø.

```
61Ø POSITION 5,4
62Ø PRINT #6;B$
```

Since we're using the POSITION command to place the text on the screen, we no longer need the PRINT statements at lines 515 and 615 which had been used originally to print blank lines in the text. Delete lines 515 and 615.

Finally we want to get rid of the previous text on the screen each time another passage of music is played. This can be done by changing lines 59Ø and 69Ø to:

```
59Ø GOTO 3Ø
69Ø GOTO 3Ø
```

In this way, once the machine has finished playing either passage, "Old" or "New," it will go back to line 3Ø and enter graphics mode 18 again. Any time you enter a new graphics mode, what was previously on the screen will be erased.

Here's a complete listing of the program:

```
Ø REM *** OLD AND NEW
1 REM *** MUZIO CLEMENTI
2 REM *** HERB MOORE
1Ø DIM A$(1Ø)
2Ø DIM B$(1Ø)
3Ø GRAPHICS 18
4Ø COLOR 1
6Ø H=INT(16*RND(1))
7Ø SETCOLOR 4,H,4

1ØØ REM *** THE STRINGS
11Ø A$="OLD MUSIC"
12Ø B$="NEW MUSIC"

2ØØ REM *** PICKS OLD OR NEW
21Ø X=INT(2*RND(1)+1)
22Ø IF X=1 THEN 51Ø
23Ø IF X=2 THEN 61Ø

5ØØ REM *** OLD SONG-CLEMENTI
51Ø POSITION 5,4
52Ø PRINT #6;A$
53Ø FOR CYCLE=1 TO 16
535 READ N
54Ø SOUND Ø,N,1Ø,1Ø
545 FOR P=1 TO 25
55Ø NEXT P
555 NEXT CYCLE
56Ø DATA 162,121,96,81
565 DATA 91,96,1Ø8,121
57Ø DATA 72,81,91,96
575 DATA 1Ø8,121,128,144
58Ø RESTORE
59Ø GOTO 3Ø

6ØØ REM *** NEW SONG-HERB + RND
61Ø POSITION 5,4
62Ø PRINT #6;B$
63Ø FOR CYCLE=1 TO 16
64Ø N=INT(25*RND(1)+1)*12
65Ø SOUND Ø,N,1Ø,1Ø
66Ø FOR P=1 TO 15
67Ø NEXT P
68Ø NEXT CYCLE
69Ø GOTO 3Ø
```

Annotations:

- Fancy print: no text window → 3Ø GRAPHICS 18
- Random hue for background screen → 7Ø SETCOLOR 4,H,4
- Places text → 51Ø POSITION 5,4
- Device #6; gives fancy print → 52Ø PRINT #6;A$ and 62Ø PRINT #6;B$
- Places text → 61Ø POSITION 5,4

Explorations

Instead of printing OLD MUSIC or NEW MUSIC, have the computer print CLEMENTI or RANDOM NOTES each time it plays a passage.

HINT: You need to change lines 110 and 120.

The string RANDOM NOTES is a little longer than the other string in the program. Change the POSITION statement in line 610 to center this string.

ENTER AND PLAY NOTES

In the remainder of this chapter, we will begin to develop a program that plays a note from the C major scale each time you enter the letter name of that note. First it will just play the note; then we'll draw a music staff and the notes will appear on the staff.

Begin by entering the following program:

```
0 REM *** NOTE PRACTICE
1 REM *** HERB MOORE
```

Dimension string →

```
10 DIM A$(5)
20 GRAPHICS 7
30 COLOR 1
40 SETCOLOR 4,11,12

100 REM *** ENTER NOTE
110 PRINT "TYPE C,D,OR E"
120 PRINT
130 PRINT "AND PRESS RETURN"
```

Assigns letter typed to string A$ →

```
140 INPUT A$

200 REM *** COMPARES STRING
```

Compares A$ tc the strings "C," "D," and "E" →

```
210 IF A$="C" THEN 310
220 IF A$="D" THEN 410
230 IF A$="E" THEN 460
290 GOTO 910
```

If A$ = "C" —

```
300 REM *** PLAYS "C"
310 N=121
350 GOSUB 2010
360 GOTO 110
```

If A$ = "D" —

```
400 REM *** PLAYS "D"
410 N=108
430 GOSUB 2010
440 GOTO 110
```

If A$ = "E"

```
450 REM *** PLAYS "E"
460 N=96
480 GOSUB 2010
490 GOTO 110
```

Some other string

```
900 REM *** INVALID CHOICE
910 PRINT "SORRY, I CAN'T PLAY"
920 PRINT A$
930 FOR P=1 TO 500
940 NEXT P
990 GOTO 110
```

Prints and plays note

```
2000 REM *** TELLS YOU THE NOTE
2010 PRINT "THIS IS THE NOTE"
2020 PRINT "YOU HAVE ENTERED"
2030 PRINT A$

3000 REM *** PLAYS THE NOTE
3010 FOR L=15 TO 0 STEP -1
3020 SOUND 0,N,10,L
3030 FOR P=1 TO 15
3040 NEXT P
3050 NEXT L
3060 RETURN
```

Now RUN the program and when the instructions appear in the text window, type C, D, or E and press RETURN.

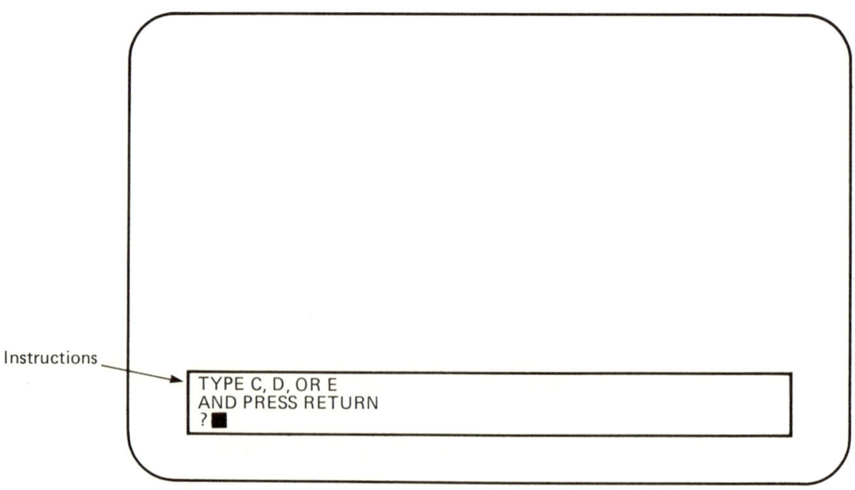

Let's say you type the letter D. Here's what should happen. The text window changes to:

while the note D is played. Then the instructions appear again on the screen.

The INPUT statement at line 14Ø gives the string A$ the value D. The IF-THEN statement at line 21Ø finds that A$ is not equal to C, so it goes on to line 22Ø. At 22Ø the conditions of the IF-THEN statement are met. That is, A$ is equal to D.

The program then branches to line 41Ø where N is given the value 1Ø8 (the value for the note D). At line 42Ø, it goes to the subroutine at line 2Ø1Ø where it prints the information telling you what note you've picked. The string D for A$ is used again here, in line 2Ø3Ø. Then in lines 3Ø1Ø through 3Ø5Ø, the note is played.

The RETURN statement at line 3Ø6Ø causes the program to pick up again at line 44Ø. Since this is a GOTO statement, it will immediately go back to line 11Ø and type the instructions again.

If you look at the blocks for the notes C,D, and E at lines 3ØØ, 4ØØ, and 45Ø respectively, you'll see that they are quite similar and work similarly in the program depending on which IF-THEN statement in lines 21Ø through 23Ø is able to find the right match for A$.

But what if you type some letter other than C,D, or E in response to the instructions when they appear in the text window? Suppose, for example, you type H. In this case none of the IF-THEN statements in lines 21Ø through 23Ø will find a match and the program will go on to line 29Ø. The GOTO statement at line 29Ø branches the program down to line 91Ø where it prints the text "SORRY, I CAN'T PLAY" along with whatever you've entered for A$. This appears in the text window. Since you've typed H, it will look like this:

RUN this program a few more times to make sure everything is working as it should, and then we'll make some additions.

Draw Staff Lines

Our goal is to have the notes appear on the music staff as they play, so add this subroutine to draw the music staff:

```
1ØØØ REM *** DRAWS MUSIC STAFF
1Ø1Ø FOR ROW=36 TO 6Ø STEP 6
1Ø2Ø PLOT 1Ø,ROW
1Ø3Ø DRAWTO 14Ø,ROW
1Ø4Ø NEXT ROW
1Ø5Ø RETURN
```

Then add line 5Ø:

```
5Ø GOSUB 1Ø1Ø
```

RUN this program now, and you should get this on the screen.

Otherwise it will operate the same as it did before. We'll add some lines to plot the notes soon, but first let's look carefully at how the staff was drawn.

Putting the GOSUB statement at line 5Ø causes the subroutine to draw the staff to be executed immediately after the graphics mode and color command have been executed.

We've used a FOR-NEXT loop for ROW. The first time through the loop, it plots a point at column 1Ø, row 36 at line 1Ø1Ø. Then at line 1Ø2Ø it draws a line to column 14Ø, row 36. That's the top line of the staff. The second time through the loop, it draws a line from column 1Ø to column 14Ø at row 42. This continues until all five staff lines are drawn. The RETURN statement at line 1Ø5Ø causes the program to pick up at line 11Ø. From there it operates the same as it did before this subroutine was added.

Make sure you have this listing before going on.

```
Ø REM *** NOTE PRACTICE
1 REM *** HERB MOORE

1Ø DIM A$(5)
2Ø GRAPHICS 7
3Ø COLOR 1
4Ø SETCOLOR 4,11,12
5Ø GOSUB 1Ø1Ø                         <-- We've added

1ØØ REM ENTER NOTE
11Ø PRINT "TYPE C,D,OR E"
12Ø PRINT
13Ø PRINT "AND PRESS RETURN"
14Ø INPUT A$

2ØØ REM *** COMPARES STRING
21Ø IF A$="C" THEN 31Ø
22Ø IF A$="D" THEN 41Ø
23Ø IF A$="E" THEN 46Ø
29Ø GOTO 91Ø

3ØØ REM *** PLAYS "C"
31Ø N=121
35Ø GOSUB 2Ø1Ø
36Ø GOTO 11Ø

4ØØ REM *** PLAYS "D"
41Ø N=1Ø8
43Ø GOSUB 2Ø1Ø
44Ø GOTO 11Ø

45Ø REM *** PLAYS "E"
46Ø N=96
48Ø GOSUB 2Ø1Ø

9ØØ REM *** INVALID CHOICE
91Ø PRINT "SORRY, I CAN'T PLAY"
92Ø PRINT A$
93Ø FOR P=1 TO 5ØØ
94Ø NEXT P
99Ø GOTO 11Ø

1ØØØ REM *** DRAWS MUSIC STAFF        ┐
1Ø1Ø FOR ROW=36 TO 6Ø STEP 6          │
1Ø2Ø PLOT 1Ø,ROW                      │ <-- We've added
1Ø3Ø DRAWTO 14Ø,ROW                   │
1Ø4Ø NEXT ROW                         │
1Ø5Ø RETURN                           ┘
```

```
2ØØØ REM *** TELLS YOU THE NOTE
2Ø1Ø PRINT "THIS IS THE NOTE"
2Ø2Ø PRINT "YOU HAVE ENTERED"
2Ø3Ø PRINT A$

3ØØØ REM *** PLAYS THE NOTE
3Ø1Ø FOR L=15 TO Ø STEP -1
3Ø2Ø SOUND Ø,N,1Ø,L
3Ø3Ø FOR P=1 TO 15
3Ø4Ø NEXT P
3Ø5Ø NEXT L
3Ø6Ø RETURN
```

Put Notes on the Staff

Rather than drawing each note on the staff separately, we can use the techniques we learned in Chapter 7 to draw a figure of the same size and shape at different places on the screen. Begin by adding the following lines to subroutine 2010:

```
2Ø4Ø REM *** DRAWS NOTE
2Ø5Ø PLOT COL,ROW
2Ø6Ø DRAWTO COL+3,ROW-3
2Ø7Ø DRAWTO COL+6,ROW
2Ø8Ø DRAWTO COL+3,ROW+3
2Ø9Ø DRAWTO COL,ROW
```

As you can see, we've made the values of both column and row variables. We want to plot in different rows depending upon the note played. This will determine on which staff line a note appears. But we want to plot the notes at equal distances from each other going from left to right across the staff. Let's start with column 15 and put notes at columns 15, 25, 35, . . . 125. This can be done with a FOR-NEXT loop for COL at lines 80 and 890. Add these lines:

```
7Ø REM ** MOVES NOTES ACROSS STAFF
8Ø FOR COL=15 TO 125 STEP 1Ø
```

and:

```
81Ø REM ** MOVES NOTES ACROSS STAFF
82Ø NEXT COL
```

Since the value for ROW will vary depending on the note played, it should be entered in the main body of the program. The block for each note played will have a different value for ROW. The note C presents some additional considerations, so we'll look at D first.

The note "D" should appear just below the bottom line of the staff. Row 63 is the appropriate row to use, so add line 420:

```
420 ROW=63
```

The appropriate ROW for E is row 60, which is right on the bottom line of the staff. Add line 470:

```
470 ROW=60
```

Now when the block for a particular note is executed, for example, line 410 through 440 for the note D, we don't want the machine to go directly back to line 110. Instead we want it to finish the FOR-NEXT loop for COL at line 810. So change line 440 and 470 to:

```
440 GOTO 810
470 GOTO 810
```

We're still ignoring the block for C, but we'll get to it soon.

Here's what we've done so far:

```
0 REM *** NOTE PRACTICE
1 REM *** HERB MOORE

10 DIM A$(5)
20 GRAPHICS 7
30 COLOR 1
40 SETCOLOR 4,11,12
50 GOSUB 1010

70 REM *** MOVES NOTE ACROSS STAFF
80 FOR COL=15 TO 125 STEP 10

100 REM ENTER NOTE
110 PRINT "TYPE C,D,OR E"
120 PRINT
130 PRINT "AND PRESS RETURN"
140 INPUT A$

200 REM *** COMPARES STRING
210 IF A$="C" THEN 310
220 IF A$="D" THEN 410
230 IF A$="E" THEN 460
290 GOTO 110

300 REM *** PLAYS "C"
310 N=121
350 GOSUB 2010
360 GOTO 110

400 REM *** PLAYS "D"
410 N=108
420 ROW=63
430 GOSUB 2010
440 GOTO 810

450 REM *** PLAYS "E"
460 N=96
470 ROW=60
480 GOSUB 2010
490 GOTO 810

800 REM *** MOVES NOTE ACROSS STAFF
810 NEXT COL
```

Puts note at next position on staff going left to right (lines 80–810)

Col value is used in 2050 through 2090

Puts note just below bottom staff line (line 420)

Next col (lines 440–490)

Puts note on bottom staff line (line 470)

```
9ØØ REM *** INVALID CHOICE
91Ø PRINT "SORRY, I CAN'T PLAY"
92Ø PRINT A$
93Ø FOR P=1 TO 5ØØ
94Ø NEXT P
99Ø GOTO 11Ø

1ØØØ REM *** DRAWS MUSIC STAFF
1Ø1Ø FOR ROW=36 TO 6Ø STEP 6
1Ø2Ø PLOT 1Ø,ROW
1Ø3Ø DRAWTO 14Ø,ROW
1Ø4Ø NEXT ROW
1Ø5Ø RETURN

2ØØØ REM *** TELLS YOU THE NOTE
2Ø1Ø PRINT "THIS IS THE NOTE"
2Ø2Ø PRINT "YOU HAVE ENTERED"
2Ø3Ø PRINT A$
```

Draws note →

```
2Ø4Ø REM *** DRAWS NOTE
2Ø5Ø PLOT COL,ROW
2Ø6Ø DRAWTO COL+3,ROW-3
2Ø7Ø DRAWTO COL+6,ROW
2Ø8Ø DRAWTO COL+3,ROW+3
2Ø9Ø DRAWTO COL,ROW

3ØØØ REM *** PLAYS THE NOTE
3Ø1Ø FOR L=15 TO Ø STEP -1
3Ø2Ø SOUND Ø,N,1Ø,L
3Ø3Ø FOR P=1 TO 15
3Ø4Ø NEXT P
3Ø5Ø NEXT L
3Ø6Ø RETURN
```

RUN this program and ENTER either D or E when the instructions appear. For the sake of illustration, let's say you enter D, E, D, D the first few times through. You should get:

As you enter each new note, it appears at the appropriate line of the staff and to the right of the previous note.

The correct position on the music staff of the note middle C is shown below:

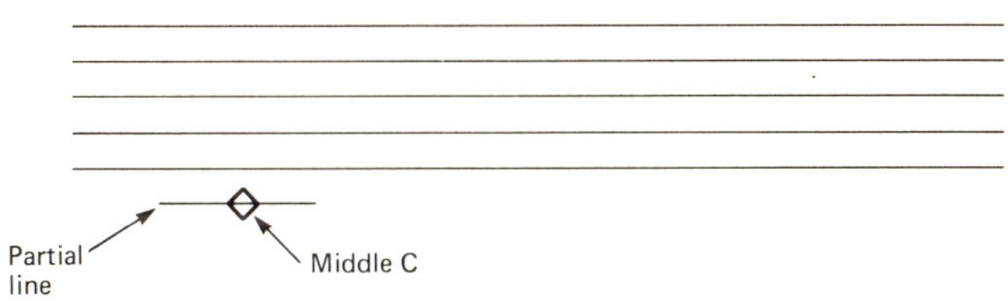

It appears one line below the bottom line of the staff and is generally shown with a partial line as it has above. So when we plot the note middle C, we want to include this partial line. This can be done by adding the following lines:

```
320 PLOT COL-1,66
330 DRAWTO COL +7,66
```

Line 360 should also be changed to:

```
360 GOTO 810
```

as in the blocks for the notes D and E.

Now if, for example, the note C is played as the first note before plotting the note, line 320 will plot a point at column 14 (that is 15 – 1), row 66, and draw a line at column 22 (15 + 7), row 66. This will draw the partial line for the note middle C. Lines 340 and 350 cause the note to be drawn just as it was drawn in the blocks for D and E. If several notes have been played before middle C is played and the FOR-NEXT loop for COL is over to column 55, for example, here's what happens. Line 32Ø and 33Ø plot and draw this:

	COL − 1	,	66
PLOT 54, 66	55 − 1	,	66
DRAWTO 62, 66	55 + 7	,	66

Make sure you've added lines 32Ø, 33Ø, and 36Ø as shown above and RUN the program. You'll now be able to ENTER C, D, or E and have the note appear on the correct staff line while it plays.

One further addition can be made to improve this program. After you've entered twelve notes, the staff will be full and the FOR-NEXT loop for COL will be finished. It would be nice to have it erase the notes and start over. Easily done. First renumber lines 8ØØ and 81Ø so they become:

```
82Ø REM ** MOVES NOTES ACROSS STAFF
83Ø NEXT COL
```

Now add lines 8ØØ and 81Ø

```
8ØØ REM * * *
81Ø IF COL=125 THEN 2Ø
```

With these lines added, each time a note is played it checks the value of COL before going on to line 83Ø for the next column. When it gets to column 125, line 81Ø goes back and enters the graphics mode again, thus erasing everything and starting over.

You may have already noticed this, but if you try to enter another note while one is playing, the computer may get a little confused and go to the invalid choice subroutine in line 91Ø. If this happens, just wait until the instruction appears in the text window and you can carry on.

Here's a complete listing of the program:

```
Ø REM *** NOTE PRACTICE
1 REM *** HERB MOORE

1Ø DIM A$(5)
2Ø GRAPHICS 7
3Ø COLOR 1
4Ø SETCOLOR 4,11,12
5Ø GOSUB 1Ø1Ø

7Ø REM *** MOVES NOTES ACROSS STAFF
8Ø FOR COL=15 TO 125 STEP 1Ø

1ØØ REM *** ENTER NOTE
11Ø PRINT "TYPE C,D,OR E"
12Ø PRINT
13Ø PRINT "AND PRESS RETURN"
14Ø INPUT A$

2ØØ REM *** COMPARES STRING
21Ø IF A$="C" THEN 31Ø
22Ø IF A$="D" THEN 41Ø
23Ø IF A$="E" THEN 46Ø
29Ø GOTO 91Ø

3ØØ REM *** PLAYS "C"
31Ø N=121
32Ø PLOT COL-1,66
33Ø DRAWTO COL+7,66
34Ø ROW=66
35Ø GOSUB 2Ø1Ø
36Ø GOTO 81Ø

4ØØ REM *** PLAYS "D"
41Ø N=1Ø8
42Ø ROW=63
43Ø GOSUB 2Ø1Ø
44Ø GOTO 81Ø

45Ø REM *** PLAYS "E"
46Ø N=96
47Ø ROW=6Ø
48Ø GOSUB 2Ø1Ø
49Ø GOTO 81Ø
```

Draws line segment below staff for middle C → (lines 32Ø–33Ø)

Checks column. If last column, start over →

```
800 REM *** IS THE STAFF FULL YET?
810 IF COL=125 THEN 20

820 REM *** MOVES NOTES ACROSS STAFF
830 NEXT COL

900 REM *** INVALID CHOICE
910 PRINT "SORRY, I CAN'T PLAY"
920 PRINT A$
930 FOR P=1 TO 500
940 NEXT P

990 GOTO 110
1000 REM *** DRAWS MUSIC STAFF
1010 FOR ROW=36 TO 60 STEP 6
1020 PLOT 10,ROW
1030 DRAWTO 140,ROW
1040 NEXT ROW
1050 RETURN

2000 REM *** TELLS YOU THE NOTE
2010 PRINT "THIS IS THE NOTE"
2020 PRINT "YOU HAVE ENTERED"
2030 PRINT A$
2039 REM
2040 REM *** DRAWS NOTE
2050 PLOT COL,ROW
2060 DRAWTO COL+3,ROW-3
2070 DRAWTO COL+6,ROW
2080 DRAWTO COL+3,ROW+3
2090 DRAWTO COL,ROW

3000 REM *** PLAYS THE NOTE
3010 FOR L=15 TO 0 STEP -1
3020 SOUND 0,N,10,L
3030 FOR P=1 TO 15
3040 NEXT P
3050 NEXT L
3060 RETURN
```

In this chapter you've learned some techniques for manipulating string variables and you've applied these techniques in beginning to build a program to put notes on a music staff.

Your challenge for this chapter is to add the remaining notes to enable the user to enter any note of the C scale from middle C to one octave above middle C. You'll need to use the note chart in Chapter 1, and you'll also need to figure the correct row for each note. Start at line 510 for the note F and model the block for each note after the blocks for D and E. Here are the notes on the staff:

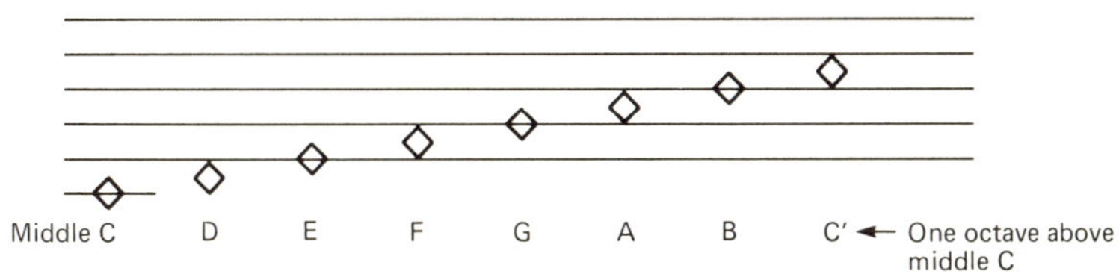

Self-Test

1. What is the minimum value that can be placed in the parentheses for this program to work?

```
10 DIM A$(      )
20 A$="SOUND SCULPTURE"
30 PRINT "SOUND SCULPTURE"
40 GOTO 30
```

2. What will this program do?

```
10 DIM Z$(100)
20 INPUT Z$
30 PRINT Z$
40 PRINT Z$
```

3. What will this program print?

```
10 DIM H$(5)
20 H$="SOUND SCULPTURE"
30 PRINT H$
```

4. What must be added to this program to have the text in lines 110 and 120 appear in the graphics display area of the screen?

```
10 GRAPHICS 2
20 COLOR 1
30 SETCOLOR 0,8,6
100 REM ***
110 PRINT "AUDITORY"
120 PRINT "TICKLE"
130 GOTO 130
```

5. In the program above, what command might you add to position the text in the center of the screen?
6. In the "Note Practice" program from this chapter, if you type H, will a note value be entered?
7. If you enter D in the "Note Practice" program, which value for N will be used in the sound statement at line 3020?
8. In the same program, if you type "SOUNDS GOOD," what will be printed at line 920?

Answers

1. 15
2. It allows you to enter a string of up to 100 characters, and then it prints that string twice.
3. It prints the word SOUND since the string H$ is only dimensioned for five characters.
4. Lines 110 and 120 must become:

```
110 PRINT #6;"AUDITORY"
120 PRINT 6; "TICKLE"
```

5. The POSITION command
6. No, because lines 300 through 490 will be skipped.
7. N will be 108 because the block at lines 410 through 440 will be executed when the conditions A$="D" are met in line 220.
8. SOUND. The rest of the string will be dropped since A$ is only dimensioned for five characters.

Challenges

1. Add a title to this program using fancy letters in the graphics display.
2. Complete the blocks for the rest of the notes in the C major scale as described at the end of the chapter.

CHAPTER TEN

Watch the Music Play

In Chapter 9 we built a program that allowed the user to ENTER the letter name of a single note. This note was then played as its position on the music staff was displayed on the screen. In this chapter we will create a program that enables you to enter a sequence of notes that the computer will keep track of in its memory. After a specified number of notes have been entered, the computer will play them back as a melody.

SUBSCRIPTED VARIABLES

A particularly useful tool for creating musical passages is the *subscripted variable,* which takes the following form:

Variable → N(4) ← Subscript

This expression is said: "N sub 4."

A subscripted variable consists of a letter (any letter from A to Z), followed by a *subscript* enclosed in parentheses.

N(4) is a subscripted variable.
N4 is not a subscripted variable.

Suppose you want to store a number of different note values in the machine's memory and use any one of these values later in the program. This can be done with a set of subscripted variables called an *array*. You can think of each note value as being stored in a box that represents a particular location in the computer's memory. For example, note values for C, E, G, and B might be represented:

N(Ø)	121
N(1)	96
N(2)	81
N(3)	64

You can have an array of more than four subscripted variables if you wish. For example, if you wanted to be able to store an array of eight possible note values, it would consist of eight memory locations in which to store note values:

N(Ø)	121
N(1)	96
N(2)	81
N(3)	64
N(4)	
N(5)	
N(6)	
N(7)	

Using the note chart from Chapter 1, add four more note values to this array to get an idea of the process by which numbers are assigned to subscripted variables.

In Chapter 9 you learned that it is necessary to use a DIM statement to reserve space in the computer's memory for the strings that were assigned to string variables. In a similar fashion, you must dimension arrays for the maximum number of values to be entered as subscripted variables.

For the array of four note values we used as our original example, you would use a DIM statement like this:

```
1Ø DIM N(3)
```

Variable for which space is being reserved (→ N)

Maximum subscript to be permitted (→ 3)

The value for the maximum subscript permitted can be greater in the above statement. For example:

```
1Ø DIM N(1Ø)
```

But if you try to use:

```
1Ø DIM N(2)
```

you'll get an ERROR message when you try to use N(3).

Before going on, see if you can answer these questions.

1. For the preceding example in which we used an array of eight subscripted variables (numbered Ø through 7), what is the smallest value you can use between the parentheses in your DIM statement?

```
1Ø DIM(?)
```

2. What is the smallest number you can use in the parentheses to dimension this array:

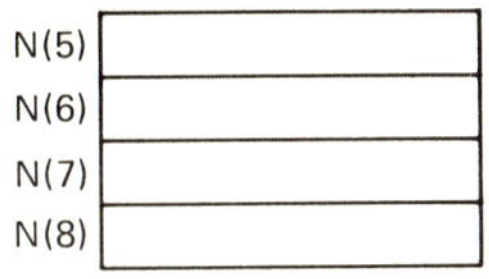

```
1. DIM(7)
2. DIM(8)
```

No matter how many subscripted variables are being used, you must dimension for the maximum subscript to be permitted.

ENTER NOTE VALUES IN AN ARRAY

Once you've dimensioned the subscript, you can use several different ways to store values for the subscripted variables in the array. Here's the long way of using subscripted variables to play the notes of the C major scale. Rather than spending a lot of time typing this, just study it carefully:

```
Ø REM *** THE LONG WAY
1Ø DIM N(8)

1ØØ REM *** ASSIGNS NOTE VALUES
1Ø1 REM *** TO SUBSCRIPTED VARIABLES
11Ø N(1)=121
12Ø N(2)=1Ø8
13Ø N(3)=96
14Ø N(4)=91
15Ø N(5)=81
16Ø N(6)=72
17Ø N(7)=64
18Ø N(8)=6Ø

2ØØ REM *** PLAYS NOTES
2Ø1 REM *** "E" IS VALUE OF SUBSCRIPT
21Ø FOR E=1 TO 8
22Ø SOUND Ø,N(E),1Ø,1Ø
23Ø FOR P=1 TO 2ØØ:NEXT P
24Ø NEXT E

3ØØ REM *** PLAY IT AGAIN
31Ø GOTO 11Ø
```

First, each of the note values in the scale is assigned to a subscripted variable in lines 110 through 180. Then as the FOR-NEXT loop in lines 210 through 240 is executed:

> When E is 1, N(E) is N(1). Its value is 121.
> When E is 2, N(E) is N(2). Its value is 108.
> And so on . . .

A more efficient way of assigning note values to subscripted variables is to use READ and DATA statements. ENTER and RUN this program and you will hear the notes of a C major scale played:

```
10 DIM N(8)
100 REM *** READS NOTE VALUES
110 FOR E=1 TO 8
120 READ N

150 REM *** PUTS NOTE VALUES IN ARRAY
160 N(E)=N
170 NEXT E

200 REM *** PLAYS NOTES
210 FOR E=1 TO 8
220 SOUND 0,N(E),10,10
230 FOR P=1 TO 200:NEXT P
240 NEXT E

300 REM *** PLAYS IT AGAIN
310 GOTO 210

400 REM *** NOTE VALUES FOR C SCALE
410 DATA 121,108,96,91
420 DATA 81,72,64,60
```

Lines 200 through 240 of this program are the same as in the previous program listing. Their operation has already been described.

Lines 110 through 180, however, have been replaced with a loop that reads note values from the DATA statement in lines 410 and 420.

The FOR-NEXT loop in lines 110 through 170 assigns values of 1 through 8 to the subscript E in line 160. At the same time the READ statement in line 120 gives N a note value from the DATA statements in lines 410 and 420. The first time through the loop E is given a value of 1 and N is given a value of 121. In line 160 we get:

```
         160 N(E)=N
Says ──→ 160 N(1)=121
```

The second time through the loop:

```
160 N(E)=N
160 N(2)=108
```

The third time:

```
160 N(E)=N
160 N(3)=96
```

In the same way that we've just demonstrated, show what values will be assigned to E and N in line 160 on the fifth and seventh time through the loop.

The fifth time through the loop:

```
160 N(E)=N
160 N(5)=81
```

The seventh time through the loop:

```
160 N(E)=N
160 N(7)=64
```

If you wish to play only a part of the scale, you can make line 210 something like:

```
210 FOR E=1 TO 5
```

which would play the first five notes. Or to play notes from the middle of the scale, line 210 might be:

```
210 FOR E=3 TO 6
```

Which note values do you think this version of line 210 will play?

96, 91, 81, and 72

You can use the STEP function to skip notes and go either up or down the scale. For example, make line 210:

```
210 FOR E=1 TO 7 STEP 2
```

and add lines:

```
250 REM *** DESCENDING LINE
260 FOR E=8 TO 2 STEP -2
270 SOUND 0,N(E),10,10
280 FOR P=1 TO 50:NEXT P
290 NEXT E
```

We've also changed the REM statement in line 200 to better describe what is happening with the new line 210:

```
200 REM ** ASCENDING LINE
```

The program listing should now be:

```
10 DIM N(8)
100 REM *** READS NOTE VALUES
110 FOR E=1 TO 8
120 READ N

150 REM *** PUTS NOTE VALUES IN ARRAY
160 N(E)=N
170 NEXT E

200 REM *** ASCENDING LINE
210 FOR E=1 TO 7 STEP 2
220 SOUND 0,N(E),10,10
230 FOR P=1 TO 50:NEXT P
240 NEXT E

250 REM *** DESCENDING LINE
260 FOR E=8 TO 2 STEP -2
270 SOUND 0,N(E),10,10
280 FOR P=1 TO 50:NEXT P
290 NEXT E

300 REM *** PLAYS IT AGAIN
310 GOTO 210

400 REM *** NOTE VALUES FOR C SCALE
410 DATA 121,108,96,91
420 DATA 81,72,64,60
```

Make sure you have the correct listing and RUN the program.

As the loop in lines 210 through 240 is executed, values for the subscripted variable used in line 220 will be N(1), N(3), N(5), and N(7). The notes played will then be:

N(1) = 121	Middle C
N(3) = 96	E
N(5) = 81	G
N(7) = 64	B

Lines 26Ø through 29Ø will come back down the scale. Replace the two question marks with the correct note values:

N(8) = 6Ø	C above middle C
N(6) = ?	A
N(4) = ?	F
N(2) = 1Ø8	D

RANDOM CHOICE OF NOTES AND DURATION

If you'd like to hear the computer make an attempt at something a little more musical than simply going up and down the scale, replace lines 2ØØ through 29Ø of the previous program with:

Randomly chooses a subscript → 21Ø

Gives notes a random duration → 22Ø, 24Ø

```
2ØØ REM *** PLAYS NOTES
21Ø E=INT(8*RND(1)+1)
22Ø DUR=INT(4*RND(1)+)*2Ø
23Ø SOUND Ø,N(E),1Ø,1Ø
24Ø FOR P=1 TO DUR:NEXT P
```

The complete listing will be:

```
1Ø DIM N(8)
1ØØ REM *** READS NOTE VALUES
11Ø FOR E=1 TO 8
12Ø READ N

15Ø REM *** PUTS NOTE VALUES IN ARRAY
16Ø N(E)=N
17Ø NEXT E

2ØØ REM *** PLAYS NOTES
21Ø E=INT(8*RND(1)+1)
22Ø DUR=INT(4*RND(1)+1)*2Ø
23Ø SOUND Ø,N(E),1Ø,1Ø
24Ø FOR P=1 TO DUR:NEXT P

3ØØ REM *** PLAYS IT AGAIN
31Ø GOTO 21Ø

4ØØ REM *** NOTE VALUES FOR C SCALE
41Ø DATA 121,1Ø8,96,91
42Ø DATA 81,72,64,6Ø
```

Line 210 randomly chooses a value for the subscript E. For the sake of illustration, let's say it picked the number 5. The subscripted variable in line 230 then becomes N(5). Since the READ and DATA statements have given N(5) a value of 81, note value 81 will be played in the sound statement.

Line 220 picks a random number from 1 to 4 and then multiplies that number by 20 to give DUR possible values of 20, 40, 60, or 80. Using the variable DUR in the pause loop in line 240 results in one of these values for the duration of the note. Keep this program because we'll add to it in a moment.

A LITTLE MUSIC THEORY

Any time you go from one note to another in a musical scale, you are playing an *interval*. For example, from D to E is an interval. Each interval has a name derived from how far you move within the scale. You name an interval by counting how many notes you jump up or down the scale. Include the note you start with and the note you finish with. For example:

C Major Scale
C, D, E, F, G, A, B, C

	Jump From	Interval Name
going up	D to E	second
going up	E to G	third
going up	F to G	second
going down	G to D	fourth
going down	B to F	fourth
going up	D to A	fifth
going down	G to E	third

The interval from any note to the note with the same name going either up or down is an *octave* of that note. From middle C to the next highest C is an octave. If you start with D and go up or down to the next D, then you are playing the octave of D.

Fill in the names of the following intervals:

	Jump From	*Interval Name*
going up	C to G	?
going down	A to F	?
going up	C to B	?
going down	B to D	?

fifth
third
seventh
sixth

We won't go into an elaborate discussion of music theory, but suffice it to say that the real building blocks for conventional harmony in our culture are thirds.

Now, looking again at the program we've been using, we can make a few changes to play in thirds.

First add:

```
25Ø SOUND 1,N(E+2),1Ø,1Ø
26Ø FOR P=1 TO DUR:NEXT P
27Ø SOUND 2,N(E+2),1Ø,1Ø
28Ø FOR P=1 TO DUR:NEXT P
```

Then change line 210 to:

```
21Ø E=INT(6*RND(1) + 1)
```

This listing should now be:

```
Ø REM *** ENDLESS SONG
1 REM *** BY HERB MOORE
2 REM *** AND THE RANDOM NOTES

1Ø DIM N(1Ø)
1ØØ REM *** READS NOTE VALUES
11Ø FOR E=1 TO 8
12Ø READ N

15Ø REM *** PUTS NOTE VALUES IN ARRAY
16Ø N(E)=N
17Ø NEXT E
18Ø RESTORE

2ØØ REM *** PLAYS NOTES
21Ø E=INT(6*RND(1)+1)
22Ø DUR=INT(4*RND(1)+1)*2Ø
23Ø SOUND Ø,N(E),1Ø,1Ø
24Ø FOR P=1 TO DUR:NEXT P
25Ø SOUND 1,N(E+2),1Ø,1Ø
26Ø FOR P=1 TO DUR:NEXT P
27Ø SOUND 2,N(E+2),1Ø,1Ø
28Ø FOR P=1 TO DUR:NEXT P

3ØØ REM *** PLAYS IT AGAIN
31Ø GOTO 21Ø

4ØØ REM *** NOTE VALUES FOR C SCALE
41Ø DATA 121,1Ø8,96,91
42Ø DATA 81,72,64,6Ø
```

RUN the program to hear the computer's idea of music for around the campfire.

Line 210 picks a subscript from 1 to 6 that is used in line 230. It was necessary to reduce the choices for E to 1 through 6 since in lines 250 and 270 we are using subscripts of E + 2.

If the subscript 4 is chosen at line 210 and then at lines 250 and 270, note value 72 (A, which is a third above F) is played.

If it picks 2 for the subscript E, you'll hear note values 108 and 91; that's the third D and F. Lines 260 and 280 give each note a random duration.

What note values are played in line 250 if the subscript E is:

Subscript E	*Note Value*
4	?
6	?
3	?
5	?

72
60
81
64

If you want someone who uses the program to be able to specify the note sequence and the duration of the notes, you can use an INPUT statement. ENTER and RUN the following program to see an example of how an INPUT statement can be used to assign values to subscripted variables:

```
10 DIM N(10)

100 REM *** ENTER NOTES IN ARRAY
110 FOR E=1 TO 8
120 PRINT "ENTER NOTE VALUE"
130 INPUT N

170 N(E)=N
190 NEXT E

200 REM *** PLAYS NOTES FROM ARRAY
210 FOR E=1 TO 8
220 DUR=INT(4*RND(1)+1)*20
230 SOUND 0,N(E),10,10
240 FOR P=1 TO DUR:NEXT P
250 NEXT E

300 REM *** PLAY NOTES AGAIN
310 GOTO 210
```

Each time through the loop in lines 11Ø through 19Ø these instructions will appear on the screen:

```
ENTER NOTE VALUE
?
```

The first time through the loop, the note value that is entered will be assigned to N(1). For example, suppose you enter 1Ø8. Here's what happens at line 17Ø:

```
17Ø N(1)=1Ø8
```

Let's say the next time the instruction appears you type 91. This time line 17Ø becomes:

```
17Ø N(2)=91
```

This will happen eight times before the melody is played, so, if you haven't done it already, add six more note values of your own choice.

After you've entered a total of eight note values, the program continues at line 21Ø, which begins a loop to play the eight notes. Line 22Ø establishes a randomly chosen duration for each note.

RUN this program again and ENTER a sequence of notes using several thirds. For example:

```
 C    E    G    F    A    C    G    B
121   96   81   91   72   6Ø   81   64
   [ ]  [ ]  [ ]  [ ]  [ ]  [ ]  [ ]
   3rd  3rd  2nd  3rd  3rd  4th  3rd
```

Explorations

Make up some sequences of mostly thirds for yourself.
Try a sequence of mostly fifths.
Try one of mostly fourths.
Mix thirds, fourths, and fifths.

Adding More Notes

You don't have to confine yourself to the eight notes we've shown. The note chart in Chapter 1 shows note values for three full octaves of the key of C, so help yourself.

If you want to be able to enter more notes, you can change lines 11Ø and 21Ø something like this:

```
11Ø FOR E=1 TO 16
21Ø FOR E=1 TO 16
```

But you'll have to change the DIM statement in line 1Ø to:

```
1Ø DIM N(16)
```

In the program as it exists now, you are able to determine the note values, but the computer selects the duration for you.

You can dimension another subscripted variable for the note duration and assign values to it in the same loop as N(E). Let's call this subscripted variable DUR(E).

Make sure you have this listing for the program to play notes:

```
1Ø DIM N(1Ø)

1ØØ REM *** ENTER NOTES IN ARRAY
11Ø FOR E=1 TO 8
12Ø PRINT "ENTER NOTE VALUE"
13Ø INPUT N

17Ø N(E)=N
19Ø NEXT E

2ØØ REM *** PLAYS NOTES FROM ARRAY
21Ø FOR E=1 TO 8
22Ø DUR=INT(4*RND(1)+1)*2Ø
23Ø SOUND Ø,N(E),1Ø,1Ø
24Ø FOR P=1 TO DUR:NEXT P
25Ø NEXT E

3ØØ REM *** PLAY NOTES AGAIN
31Ø GOTO 21Ø
```

Now add:

```
2Ø DIM DUR(1Ø)
14Ø PRINT "ENTER DURATION"
15Ø INPUT DUR
18Ø DUR(E)=DUR
```

And remove line 22Ø.

We've added a REM statement for clarification at line 160.

```
160 REM *** SUBSCRIPTED VARIABLES
```

The complete listing should now be:

```
10 DIM N(10)
20 DIM DUR(10)

100 REM *** ENTER NOTES IN ARRAY
110 FOR E=1 TO 8
120 PRINT "ENTER NOTE VALUE"
130 INPUT N
140 PRINT "ENTER DURATION"
150 INPUT DUR

160 REM *** SUBSCRIPTED VARIABLES
170 N(E)=N
180 DUR(E)=DUR
190 NEXT E
200 REM *** PLAYS NOTES FROM ARRAY
210 FOR E=1 TO 8
230 SOUND 0,N(E),10,10
240 FOR P=1 TO DUR(E):NEXT P
250 NEXT E

300 REM *** PLAY NOTES AGAIN
310 GOTO 210
```

Now when you run the program, you'll have the opportunity to enter a note value and a duration for each note. For example, suppose the first time through the loop you ENTER 96 for the note value when the instruction:

```
ENTER NOTE VALUE
```

appears on the screen.

Then when you see:

```
ENTER DURATION
```

you ENTER the value 100.

At line 170, a value of 96 is assigned to N(1), and at line 180 a value of 100 is assigned to DUR(1).

```
170 N(E)=DUR
```

becomes:

```
170 N(1)=96
```

and:

```
180 DUR(E)=DUR
```

becomes:

```
180 DUR(1)=100
```

Suppose the next time through the loop you enter 60 for the note value and 50 for the duration. What will happen at line 170 and 180?

```
170 N(E)=N
```

becomes:

```
170 ?
```

and:

```
180 DUR(E)=DUR
```

becomes:

```
180 ?
```

```
170 N(2)=60
180 DUR (2)=50
```

We'll leave it to you to compose melodies you like with this program. Remember you can increase the maximum value of the subscript in the DIM statement in lines 10 and 20 and then make the 8 in lines 110 and 120 a larger number if you want to play more notes.

USING STRING VARIABLES WITH AN ARRAY

You've learned how to assign note values to subscripted variables in an array and have the computer play the notes back for you either randomly or in the order that you ENTER them. But rather than having to look up the note values in the chart each time, it would be convenient to be able to ENTER the letter name of a note.

The following program lets you type a C, D, or E and assigns the note value for that letter to a subscripted variable:

```
1Ø DIM N(8)
2Ø DIM A$(5)

1ØØ REM *** ENTERS NOTES IN ARRAY
11Ø FOR Z=1 TO 8
12Ø INPUT A$

2ØØ REM *** FROM A LETTER TO A NUMBER
21Ø IF A$="C" THEN N=121
22Ø IF A$="D" THEN N=1Ø8
23Ø IF A$="E" THEN N=96

3ØØ REM *** SUBSCRIPTED VARIABLE
31Ø N(Z)=N

35Ø REM *** NEXT SUBSCRIPT
36Ø NEXT Z

4ØØ REM *** PLAYS THE NOTES
41Ø FOR Z=1 TO 8
43Ø SOUND Ø,N(Z),1Ø,1Ø
44Ø FOR P=1 TO 1ØØ:NEXT P
45Ø NEXT Z

5ØØ REM *** PLAY IT AGAIN
51Ø GOTO 41Ø
```

ENTER and RUN this program and type C, D, or E each time the question mark and the cursor appear on the screen.

```
? ■
```

After you ENTER eight notes, the computer will play them back for you.

Line 10 dimensions a variable with a maximum subscript of 8. Line 20 dimensions a string variable. Lines 110 through 360 form a loop similar to the ones we've been using. This loop assigns values to the subscript E in line 310.

Suppose you type the letter D the first time through the loop. At line 120 the string variable A$ becomes "D." As the computer goes through the IF-THEN statements in lines 210 through 230, it finds A$="D" in line 220. It then assigns N a value of 108. In line 310 we get:

```
310 N(Z)=N
```

becomes:

```
310 N(1)=108
```

What will happen if you type C the second time through the loop? Line 310 becomes:

```
310 N(2)=121
```

Using the note chart from Chapter 1, add IF-THEN statements at line 240 through 280 that will allow you to ENTER the notes F, G, A, B, and the octave C^1 when the program is over.

The program listing will look like this:

```
1Ø DIM N(8)
2Ø DIM A$(5)

1ØØ REM *** ENTERS NOTES IN ARRAY
11Ø FOR Z=1 TO 8
12Ø INPUT A$

2ØØ REM *** FROM A LETTER TO A NUMBER
21Ø IF A$="C" THEN N=121
22Ø IF A$="D" THEN N=1Ø8
23Ø IF A$="E" THEN N=96
24Ø IF A$="F" THEN N=91
25Ø IF A$="G" THEN N=81
26Ø IF A$="A" THEN N=72
27Ø IF A$="B" THEN N=64
28Ø IF A$="C1" THEN N=6Ø

3ØØ REM *** SUBSCRIPTED VARIABLE
31Ø N(Z)=N

35Ø REM *** NEXT SUBSCRIPT
36Ø NEXT Z

4ØØ REM *** PLAYS THE NOTES
41Ø FOR Z=1 TO 8
43Ø SOUND Ø,N(Z),1Ø,1Ø
44Ø FOR P=1 TO 1ØØ:NEXT P
45Ø NEXT Z

5ØØ REM *** PLAY IT AGAIN
51Ø GOTO 41Ø
```

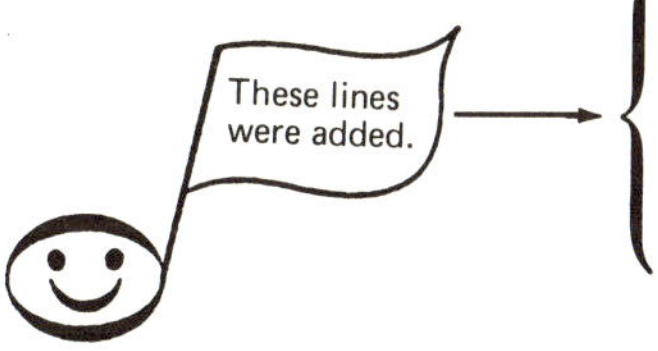

Now RUN the program and make up some note sequences from all eight notes.

MAKE YOUR OWN MELODY

In Chapter 9 you learned how to have each note play and appear on the music staff immediately after it was entered. The following program uses many of the same concepts. But this time, as the letter for each note is typed, the note value for that letter is assigned to a subscripted variable and stored in an array. You are also able to determine the duration of each note. After ten notes, each with a specific duration, have been entered, the entire melody is played and shown on the staff as it plays. This will repeat until you stop the run. Then you can ENTER another melody.

This may seem like a fair amount of typing, but it will be valuable to you to take the time to ENTER this program, both for the sake of your computer education as well as the fun of making your own melody.

```
Ø REM *** MAKE A MELODY
1 REM -=- HERB MOORE
1Ø REM *** STRING VARIABLE
2Ø DIM A$(5)
```

Dimension subscripted variable for *note*, *duration*, and *row* →

```
3Ø REM *** SUBSCRIPTED VARIABLES
4Ø DIM N(1Ø)
5Ø DIM DUR(1Ø)
6Ø DIM ROW(1Ø)
```

Subroutine to enter graphics mode and draw staff →

```
7Ø REM *** DOES GRAPHICS
8Ø GOSUB 1Ø1Ø
```

For-next loop to assign values to subscripted variables

```
1ØØ REM *** ENTERS NOTES IN ARRAY
11Ø FOR Z=1 TO 1Ø
12Ø PRINT "TYPE C, D, E, F"
13Ø PRINT "G, A, B, OR C1"
14Ø INPUT A$

2ØØ REM *** FROM A LETTER TO A NUMBER
21Ø IF A$="C" THEN 31Ø
215 IF A$="D" THEN 32Ø
22Ø IF A$="E" THEN 33Ø
225 IF A$="F" THEN 34Ø
23Ø IF A$="G" THEN 35Ø
235 IF A$="A" THEN 36Ø
24Ø IF A$="B" THEN 37Ø
245 IF A$="C1" THEN 38Ø
29Ø GOTO 91Ø
```

Gives letter a note value and a row value

```
3ØØ REM *** VALUES FOR NOTE AND ROW
31Ø N=121:ROW=66
315 GOTO 51Ø
32Ø N=1Ø8:ROW=63
325 GOTO 51Ø
33Ø N=96:ROW=6Ø
335 GOTO 51Ø
34Ø N=91:ROW=57
345 GOTO 51Ø

35Ø N=81:ROW=54
355 GOTO 51Ø
36Ø N=72:ROW=51
365 GOTO 51Ø
37Ø N=64:ROW=48
375 GOTO 51Ø
38Ø N=6Ø:ROW=45
385 GOTO 51Ø
```

Assigns note value to subscripted variable

Assigns row to subscripted variable

```
5ØØ REM *** SUBSCRIPTED VARIABLES
51Ø N(Z)=N
52Ø ROW(Z)=ROW
53Ø PRINT "TYPE 1 TO 4 FOR DURATION"
54Ø PRINT "1 IS A SHORT DURATION"
55Ø PRINT "4 IS A LONG DURATION"
```

Assigns duration to subscripted variable

```
56Ø REM *** ASSIGN DURATION
57Ø INPUT DUR
58Ø DUR(Z)=DUR*25
59Ø NEXT Z
```

Moves column with each new subscript (→ line 63Ø)

From line 52Ø (→ line 64Ø)

Middle C needs extra staff line (→ lines 65Ø, 81Ø–84Ø)

Loop to play notes (lines 6ØØ–68Ø)

```
6ØØ REM *** PLAYS THE NOTES
61Ø FOR Z=1 TO 1Ø
62Ø SOUND Ø,N(Z),1Ø,1Ø
63Ø COL=12*Z
64Ø ROW=ROW(Z)
65Ø IF N(Z)=121 THEN 81Ø
66Ø GOSUB 2Ø1Ø
67Ø FOR P=1 TO DUR(Z):NEXT P
68Ø NEXT Z

7ØØ REM *** PLAYS IT AGAIN
71Ø GOSUB 1Ø1Ø
79Ø GOTO 61Ø

8ØØ REM *** STAFF LINE FOR MIDDLE C
81Ø PLOT COL-1,66
82Ø DRAWTO COL+7,66
83Ø ROW=66
84Ø GOTO 66Ø
```

Wrong letter (lines 91Ø–98Ø)

```
9ØØ REM *** INCORRECT LETTER
91Ø SOUND Ø,1Ø,2,1Ø
92Ø FOR P=1 TO 25:NEXT P
93Ø SOUND Ø,Ø,Ø,Ø,
94Ø PRINT "SORRY, I CAN"T PLAY"
95Ø PRINT A$
96Ø PRINT "WAIT FOR NEXT INSTRUCTION"
97Ø FOR P=1 TO 4ØØ:NEXT P
98Ø GOTO 12Ø
```

Graphics mode and staff (lines 1Ø1Ø–1Ø9Ø)

```
1ØØØ REM *** SET UP GRAPHICS
1Ø1Ø GRAPHICS 7
1Ø2Ø COLOR 1
1Ø3Ø SETCOLOR 4,11,12
1Ø4Ø REM *** DRAWS STAFF
1Ø5Ø FOR ROW=36 TO 6Ø STEP 6
1Ø6Ø PLOT 1Ø,ROW
1Ø7Ø DRAWTO 14Ø,ROW
1Ø8Ø NEXT ROW
1Ø9Ø RETURN
```

Draws notes (lines 2Ø1Ø–2Ø9Ø)

```
2ØØØ REM *** DRAWS NOTE
2Ø1Ø PLOT COL,ROW
2Ø2Ø DRAWTO COL+3,ROW-3
2Ø3Ø DRAWTO COL+6,ROW
2Ø4Ø DRAWTO COL +3,ROW+3
2Ø5Ø DRAWTO COL,ROW
2Ø9Ø RETURN
```

In the beginning, the program dimensions a string variable at line 10 so you can enter for the note.

At lines 40 through 60, subscripted variables for note, duration, and row are dimensioned. Line 80 executes a subroutine to enter a graphics mode and draw the music staff.

The FOR-NEXT loop in lines 110 through 490 will assign values to each of the three subscripted variables we are using in the program. For example, let's say when the instructions to type a letter appear in the text window, you type the letter F. A$ will then become "F" at line 140. Then at line 225 the IF-THEN statement will branch the program to line 340, where N is given a value of 91 and ROW is given a value of 57.

At lines 510 and 520, these values are assigned to subscripted variables:

```
510 N(Z)=N
```

becomes:

```
510 N(1)=91
```

and:

```
520 ROW(Z)=ROW
```

becomes

```
520 ROW(1)=57
```

Then the instructions to type a number for duration appear in the text window. Suppose you type a 3 here. Line 570 becomes:

```
570 DUR(Z)=DUR*25
570 DUR(1)=3*25
```

or:

```
570 DUR(1)=75
```

Finally, line 580 goes back and picks the next subscript. To check your understanding of this program, answer the following questions:

1. If the second time through the loop in lines 110 through 490 you type "B", which IF-THEN statement will find a match and branch to another line?
2. After N and ROW have been given numeric values at line 370, what will happen at line 510 and 520?
3. If you type 4 for the duration when the instructions appear, what will be the value of DUR(2) in line 570?

1. Line 240 will branch to line 370
2. 510 N(Z) = N
   520 N(2) = 64
   520 ROW(Z) = ROW
   520 ROW(2) = 48
3. 570 DUR(2) = 100

Once you've entered ten notes, with a duration for each one, the entire sequence is played by the loop from 610 to 710.

Since we have entered "F" for N(1), the SOUND statement in line 610 will play a note value of 91 the first time through the loop. At line 630 COL is given a value multiplying 12 times the subscript Z, in this case:

```
12 * 1 = 12
```

Row (1) has already been given the value 57 at line 340. Since N(1) does not equal 121, line 650 will be ignored. Line 660 goes down to the subroutine at line 2020, which draws the note at column 12, row 57. It returns to line 660, which goes back to line 610 and picks the next value for the subscript Z; that is (2). Again, to check your understanding, answer these questions:

1. Since we typed "B" for the second note, what will happen at line 620?
2. What will happen to ROW (2) in line 540?
3. Since this is the second time through the loop and Z has a value of 2, what will be the value assigned the COL in line 630?

1. Line 620 will play a note value of 64
2. 640 ROW(2) = 48
3. 630 COL = 24

Remember that middle C requires a line below the staff. Suppose on the third time through the loop you type "C" for the note. In this case, N is given a value of 121 and N(3) becomes 121 in line 510. Then when the loop to play the notes is being executed in lines 610 through 680, the conditions of the IF-THEN decision in line 650 will be met. That is, N(3) does equal 121, so the program branches to line 710 and executes the routine to draw a line below the staff. It then goes back to line 660 and continues as before.

If you type some letter other than C through C^1 for the note, none of the conditions in the IF-THEN statements in lines 210 through 245 will be met. Thus 290 will branch the program to line 910 and execute the "Incorrect Letter" routine there. It then goes back to line 120 and lets you try again.

Line 610 begins the loop to play the notes. Once all ten notes have played, line 710 executes the subroutine to enter the graphics mode, again drawing the staff and thereby erasing everything else on the screen. When the computer returns to line 610, it repeats the melody and the notes.

In this chapter, you have learned to assign values for notes and plot points to a group of subscripted variables, called an array. The subscripted variables can then be used to play different sequences of notes and draw them on the music staff. This is just one example of how an array of subscripted variables might be used. Another possible use is suggested in the challenges at the end of the Self-Test this chapter.

If you've worked your way carefully through this book, you have undoubtedly begun to realize the enormous potential of your ATARI 400 or 800 Computer as an artistic and musical instrument. We hope you will find yourself returning to the pages of this book again and again for ideas you can expand upon in your own way.

Artistic programming, like many things, is something you can enjoy more as you get better. And of course, the better you get, the more you'll enjoy.

Self-Test

1. Give the following program an appropriate DIM statement at line 10 to store the eight notes in an array and play them:

```
100 REM *** READS NOTE VALUES
110 FOR E=1 TO 8
120 READ N

150 REM *** PUTS NOTE VALUES IN ARRAY
160 N(E)=N
170 NEXT E

200 REM *** PLAYS NOTES
210 FOR E=1 TO 8
220 SOUND 0,N(E),10,10
230 FOR P=1 TO 200:NEXT P
240 NEXT E

300 REM *** PLAYS IT AGAIN
310 GOTO 210
400 REM *** NOTE VALUES FOR C SCALE
410 DATA 121,108,96,91
420 DATA 81,72,64,60
```

2. As the note values are being read from the DATA statements in the above program, what value will be assigned to the subscripted variable N(4) in line 160?

3. Add another FOR-NEXT loop at lines 26Ø through 29Ø to play note values:

N(7)	N(5)	N(3)	N(1)
64	81	96	121

in that order.

4. If rather than reading the note values into the array, you wish the user to be able to enter values for each subscripted variables, you can drop lines 4ØØ through 42Ø, and change line 12Ø to:

    12Ø________________

5. In the program in Question 1, to have the computer randomly select from the note values in the DATA statements, drop line 24Ø and change line 21Ø to:

    21Ø________________

6. Fill in line 18Ø in the program below to assign values to the subscripted variables for duration:

```
1Ø DIM N(1Ø)
2Ø DIM DUR(1Ø)

1ØØ REM *** ENTER NOTES IN ARRAY
11Ø FOR E=1 TO 8
12Ø PRINT "ENTER NOTE VALUE"
13Ø INPUT N
14Ø PRINT "ENTER DURATION"
15Ø INPUT DUR

16Ø REM *** SUBSCRIPTED VARIABLES
17Ø N(E)=N
18Ø
19Ø NEXT E

2ØØ REM *** PLAYS NOTES FROM ARRAY
21Ø FOR E=1 TO 8
23Ø SOUND Ø,N(E),1Ø,1Ø
24Ø FOR P=1 TO DUR(E):NEXT P
25Ø NEXT E

3ØØ REM *** PLAY NOTES AGAIN
31Ø GOTO 21Ø
```

7. If you wish to enter and play sixteen notes in the following program, you must change three lines. What changes must you make?

```
10 DIM N(8)
20 DIM A$(5)

100 REM ** ENTERS NOTES IN ARRAY
110 FOR Z=1 TO 8
120 INPUT A$

200 REM ** FROM A LETTER TO A NUMBER
210 IF A$="C" THEN N=121
220 IF A$="D" THEN N=108
230 IF A$="E" THEN N=96
240 IF A$="F" THEN N=91
250 IF A$="G" THEN N=81
260 IF A$="A" THEN N=72
270 IF A$="B" THEN N=64
280 IF A$="C1" THEN N=60

300 REM ** SUBSCRIPTED VARIABLE
310 N(Z)=N

400 REM ** PLAYS THE NOTES
410 FOR Z=1 TO 8
430 SOUND 0,N(Z),10,10
440 FOR P=1 TO 100:NEXT P
450 NEXT Z

500 REM ** PLAY IT AGAIN
510 GOTO 410
```

8. If when the program above is run, you type the letter "D" for the first note and the letter "F" for the second note, what musical interval have you played?

Answers

1. Line 10 becomes:

```
10 DIM N(8)
```

The subscript in parentheses can be greater than 8 but not smaller.

2. 91

3. Something of this form:

```
26Ø FOR E=7 TO 1 STEP -2
27Ø SOUND Ø,N(E),1Ø,1Ø
28Ø FOR P=1 TO 2ØØ:NEXT P
29Ø NEXT E
```

4.
```
INPUT N
```

5. Line 21Ø should be:

```
21Ø E = INT(8*RND(1) +1)
```

6. Line 18Ø becomes:

```
18Ø DUR(E) = DUR
```

7. Change lines 1Ø, 11Ø, and 41Ø to:

```
1Ø DIM N(16)
11Ø FOR Z = 1 TO 16
41Ø FOR Z = 1 TO 16
```

8. A third

Challenges

1. Here are the note values and row positions of four more notes in the next octave of the C major scale. Continue the pattern established in lines 21Ø through 385 to assign the values for note and row to subscripted variables. Then RUN the program and enjoy a wider range of notes from which to make your melody.

	D1	E1	F1	G1
Note Value	53	47	45	4Ø
Row Value	42	39	36	33

2. Look at Chapter 5 and see if you can think of some interesting ways to change the shape of the notes as they are played.
3. Draw a mountain range similar to the one in Chapter 8 using an array of subscripted variables for the mountain peaks.

APPENDIX A

Here are a few program listings that make use of concepts you have learned in this book. Some of them might be useful to you as subroutines in larger programs you are writing. We encourage you to vary different parameters in each of these programs and to write other programs that expand upon these ideas.

You know best what you want to see and hear and if you persist, you'll probably be able to make it happen!

This program randomly picks and plays a note value from 25 to 250. Try it with 25 notes from elsewhere in the note spectrum. (See Chapter 8.)

```
100 REM *** FLIGHT OF THE HONEY BEE
110 N=INT(25*RND(1)+225)
120 SOUND 0,N,10,10
130 FOR P=1 TO 5
140 NEXT P
150 GOTO 110
```

Enter a number from 0 to 255 to hear different machine sounds. Add a pause loop between lines 230 and 260 to get a slower machine sound.

```
0 REM *** MACHINE SOUND
10 INPUT N
110 FOR CYCLE=1 TO 100
210 FOR L=15 TO 0 STEP -5
220 SOUND 0,N,4,L
230 SOUND 1,N,8,L
260 NEXT L
310 NEXT CYCLE
510 GOTO 10
```

If this routine doesn't give you just the right sound for your space game, play around with the values for N, L, and STEP in lines 110 and 120. Don't forget to use INPUT statements to make it easy on yourself. (See Chapter 5.)

```
100 REM *** STUCK IN SPACE
110 FOR N=100 TO 140 STEP 5
120 FOR L=5 TO 15 STEP 5
130 SOUND 0,N,10,L
140 SOUND 1,N/2,10,15-L
150 SOUND 2,N/4,10,L
160 SOUND 3,N/8,10,15-L
170 NEXT L
180 NEXT N
190 GOTO 110
```

The following program allows you to ENTER a note value. It then plays that note and its octave with voices 0 and 2. Voices 1 and 3, meanwhile, play a note just slightly lower than N and it's octave N/2. This creates the pulsing sound heard when the program is run. The pulses are called "beat frequencies" or simply "beats."

```
50 INPUT N
100 REM ** PHASE SHIFT
120 SOUND 0,N,10,10
130 SOUND 1,N+1,10,10
140 SOUND 2,N/2,10,10
150 SOUND 3,N/2+1,10,10
210 GOTO 210
```

To hear an interesting sequence of "beats," ENTER and RUN this program, which is similar to the one above but enters the values for N with a FOR-NEXT loop. Can you think of a way to use the same concept with READ and DATA statements to ENTER the note values? How about with subscripted variables in an array?

```
100 REM ** PHASE SHIFT
110 FOR N=50 TO 250 STEP 10
120 SOUND 0,N,10,10
130 SOUND 1,N+1,10,10
140 SOUND 2,N/2,10,10
150 SOUND 3,N/2+1,10,10
160 FOR P=1 TO 1000:NEXT P
170 NEXT N
210 GOTO 110
```

This program creates a nice visual effect as it is being drawn, as well as when it is completed. Get some variety by changing the STEP function in line 110.

```
0 REM *** MANDALA
10 GRAPHICS 24
20 COLOR 1
30 SETCOLOR 4,4,8
100 REM *** DRAWS THE LINES
110 FOR ROW=10 TO 180 STEP 10
120 COL=150
130 PLOT 0,90
140 DRAWTO COL,ROW
150 PLOT 319,90
160 DRAWTO COL,ROW
190 NEXT ROW
200 REM *** KEEPS IT ON SCREEN
210 GOTO 210
```

Here's another program that's fun to watch being drawn as it fills the screen with little diamonds. Some interesting variations can be created by making changes in the STEP functions in lines 110 and 120. Also try different figures in lines 210 through 320.

```
0 REM *** DIAMOND GRID
10 GRAPHICS 24
20 COLOR 1
30 SETCOLOR 2,0,2
100 REM *** LOOPS TO REPEAT FIGURE
110 FOR COL=10 TO 300 STEP 10
120 FOR ROW=10 TO 180 STEP 10
200 REM *** DRAWS THE DIAMOND
210 PLOT COL,ROW
220 DRAWTO COL+5,ROW-5
230 DRAWTO COL+10,ROW
240 DRAWTO COL+5,ROW+5
250 DRAWTO COL,ROW
300 REM *** MOVES TO NEXT POSITION
310 NEXT ROW
320 NEXT COL
400 REM *** KEEPS IT ON SCREEN
410 GOTO 410
```

The following program uses two different FOR-NEXT loops, each of which calls on the same subroutine to draw a series of different-sized squares. Try it with some different figures.

```
1 REM ** COLOR SQUARES
10 GRAPHICS 24
20 COLOR 1
40 SETCOLOR 4,4,14
100 REM *** SMALL SQUARES
110 FOR X=1 TO 50 STEP 10
120 A=50
130 GOSUB 600
140 NEXT X
150 FOR Z=1 TO 100:NEXT Z
200 REM *** LARGE SQUARES
210 FOR X=5 TO 95 STEP 20
220 A=100
230 GOSUB 600
240 NEXT X
250 FOR Z=1 TO 500:NEXT Z
300 REM *** STARTS AGAIN
310 GOTO 10
600 REM *** DRAWS SQUARES
610 Y=X
620 PLOT X,Y
630 DRAWTO X+A,Y
640 DRAWTO X+A,Y+A
650 DRAWTO X,Y+A
660 DRAWTO X,Y
670 RETURN
```

If you like the "echo effect" often used by John Lennon in his recordings, you'll probably appreciate the sound made by this program. By briefly turning the voice on and off in lines 210 through 240, just before the decay loop starts, an echo is created.

```
Ø REM *** ECHO EFFECT
1ØØ REM *** READ NOTES
11Ø FOR CYCLE=1 TO 8
12Ø READ N
2ØØ REM *** PLAYS NOTE WITH ECHO
21Ø SOUND Ø,N,1Ø,15
22Ø FOR P=1 TO 5:NEXT P
23Ø SOUND Ø,Ø,Ø,Ø
24Ø FOR P=1 TO 5:NEXT P
249 REM
25Ø FOR L=15 TO Ø STEP -1
26Ø SOUND Ø,N,1Ø,L
27Ø NEXT L
3ØØ REM *** PLAYS ANOTHER NOTE
31Ø NEXT CYCLE
32Ø RESTORE
4ØØ REM *** STARTS OVER
41Ø GOTO 11Ø
5ØØ REM *** THE NOTE VALUES
51Ø DATA 91,121,72,64
52Ø DATA 121,81,6Ø,121
```

APPENDIX B

Values for Musical Notes*

	Note	Numeric Value
High notes	C	29
	B	31
	A# or B♭	33
	A	35
	G# or A♭	37
	G	40
	F# or G♭	42
	F	45
	E	47
	D# or E♭	50
	D	53
	C# or D♭	57
	C	60
	B	64
	A# or B♭	68
	A	72
	G# or A♭	76
	G	81
	F# or G♭	85
	F	91
	E	96
	D# or E♭	102
	D	108
	C# or D♭	114
Middle C	C	121
	B	128
	A# or B♭	136
	A	144
	G# or A♭	153
	G	162
	F# or G♭	173
	F	182
	E	193
	D# or E♭	204
Low notes	D	217
	C# or D♭	230
	C	243

*From the *ATARI 400/800™ BASIC Reference Manual*, page 58.

APPENDIX C

Plot Points for ATARI Graphics Modes

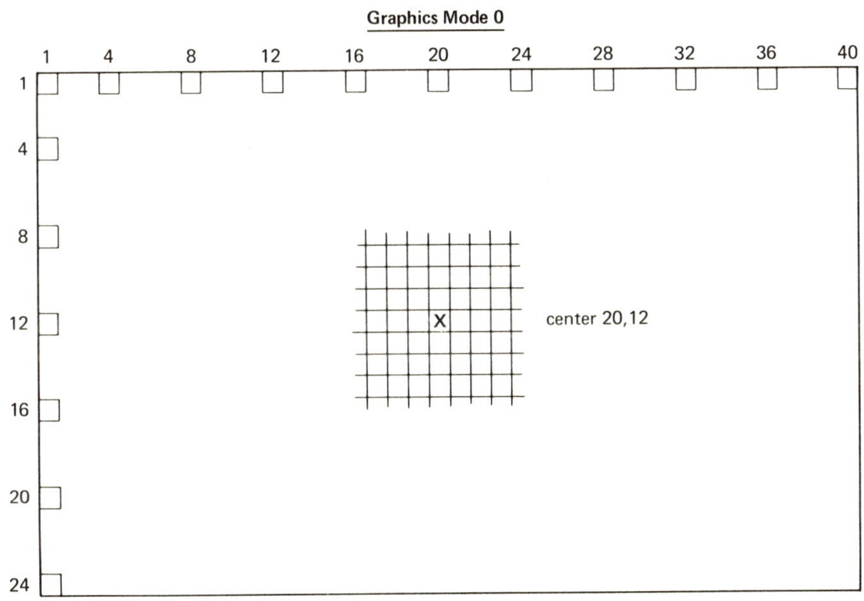

NOTES: *Text Mode – When the machine is turned on, it is in Graphics Mode 0 until otherwise specified.*

ATARI TECHNICAL SERVICES

Graphics Mode 1

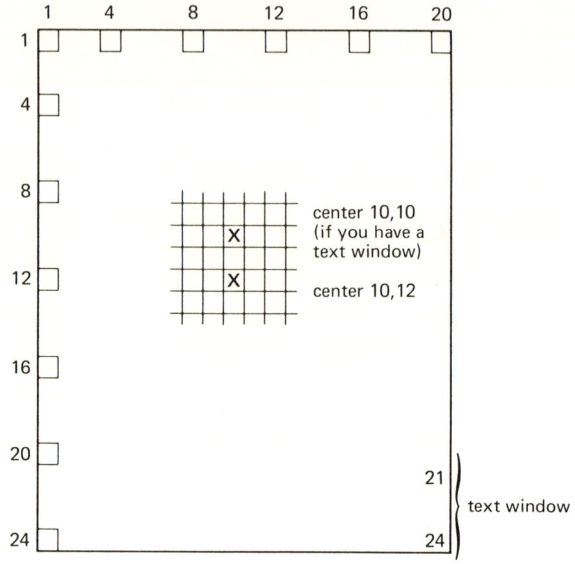

NOTES: *Text Mode for large colored letters. You must use device #6. (See Chapter 9)*

ATARI TECHNICAL SERVICES

Graphics Mode 2

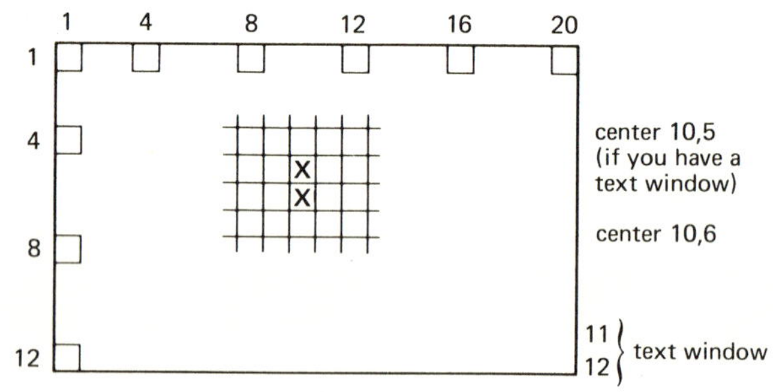

NOTES: *Text Mode for colored letters. You must use device #6. (see Chapter 9)*

ATARI TECHNICAL SERVICES

Graphics Mode 3

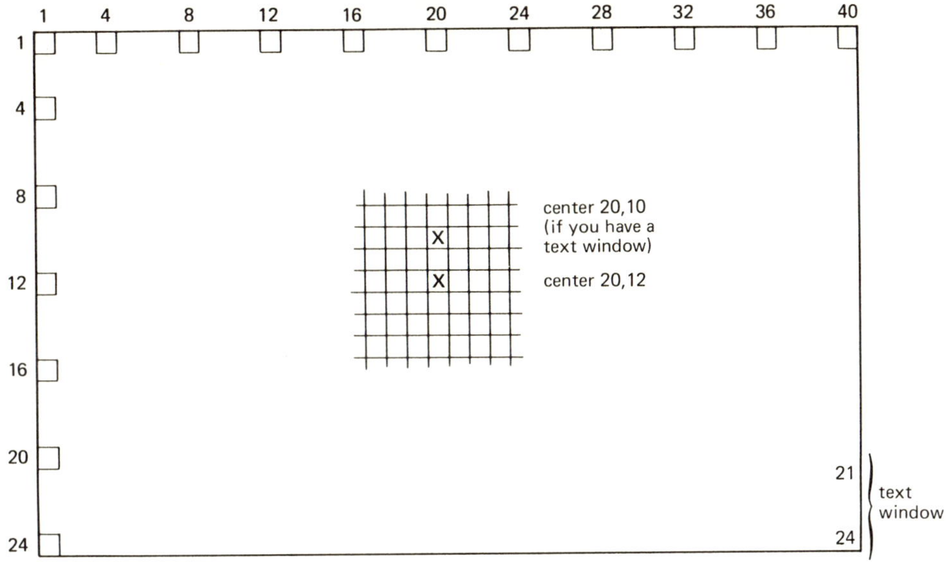

NOTES: *For same size plot points without text window, use GRAPHICS 3 + 16.*

ATARI TECHNICAL SERVICES

Graphics Mode 4

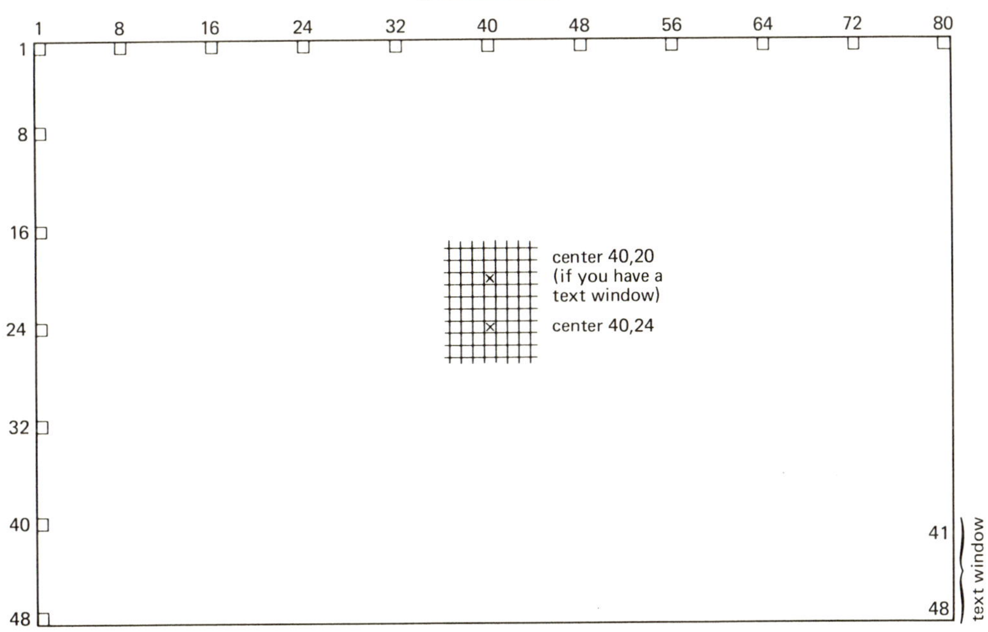

NOTES: *For same size plot points without text window, use GRAPHICS 4 + 16.*

ATARI TECHNICAL SERVICES

Graphics Mode 5

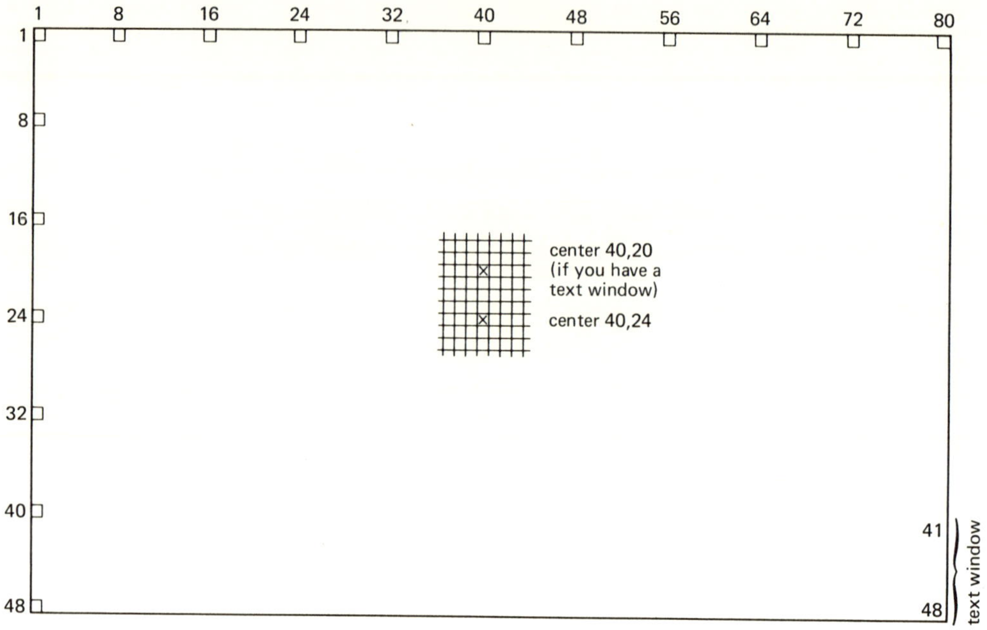

NOTES: *For same size plot points without text window, use GRAPHICS 5 + 16.*

ATARI TECHNICAL SERVICES

Graphics Mode 6

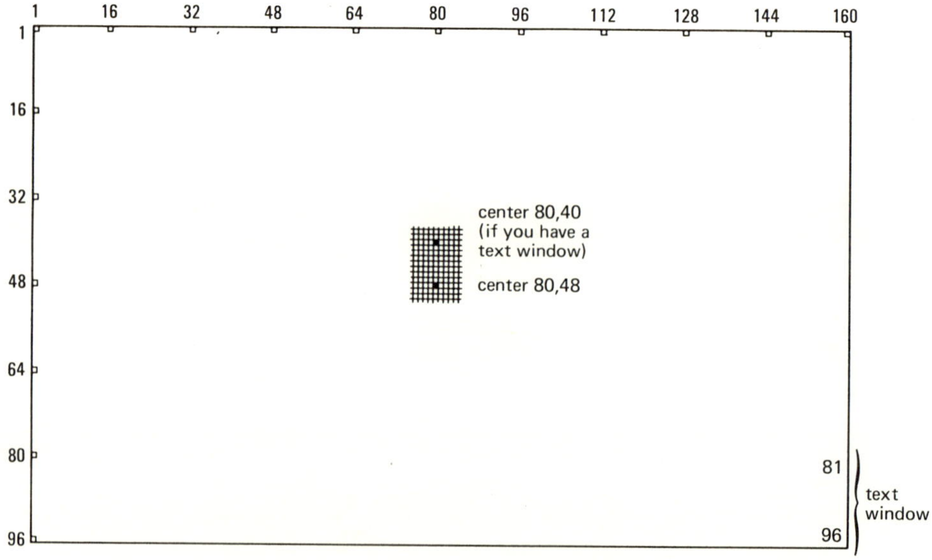

NOTES: *For same size plot points without text window, use GRAPHICS 6 + 16.*

ATARI TECHNICAL SERVICES

Graphics Mode 7

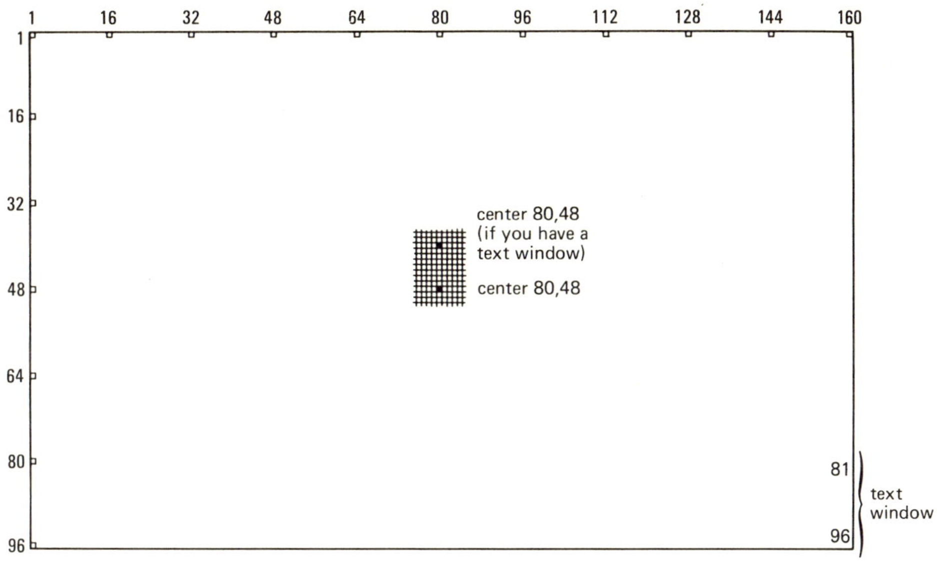

NOTES: *For same size plot points without text window, use GRAPHICS 7 + 16.*

ATARI TECHNICAL SERVICES

Graphics Mode 8

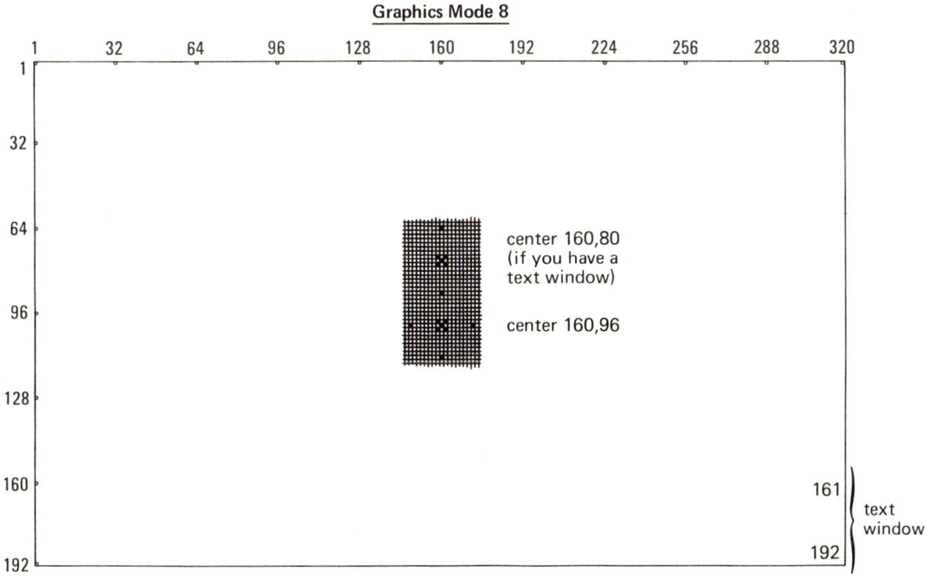

NOTES:

ATARI TECHNICAL SERVICES

APPENDIX D

Graphics Mode 1 and 2 (Text Modes With Fancy Letters)

Value for COLOR command	Value for Color Register	RESULTS ON SCREEN: Letters on display screen	Background screen	Text window
Ø	Ø	Changes hue	Dark grey	Dark blue
	1	Orange	"	"
	2	"	"	Changes hue
	3	"	"	Dark blue
	4	"	Changes hue	"
1 (Same as COLOR Ø)	Ø			
	1			
	2			
	3			
	4			
2 (Same as COLOR Ø)	Ø			
	1			
	2			
	3			
	4			
3 (Same as COLOR Ø)	Ø			
	1			
	2			
	3			
	4			
4 (Same as COLOR Ø)	Ø			
	1			
	2			
	3			
	4			

NOTE: A single color listed in the third, fourth, or fifth column indicates the default color for that combination of COLOR and Color Register. For example, in graphics mode 3, a combination of COLOR 1 and Color Register 2 will result in the figure remaining orange, regardless of the value entered for Hue in the SETCOLOR command.

Graphics Mode 3, 5, 7

Value for COLOR command	Value for Color Register	RESULTS ON SCREEN: Plot points or figure	Background screen	Text window
	Ø	Defaults to color of background	Dark grey	Dark blue
Ø	1	"	"	"
	2	"	"	Changes hue
	3	"	"	Dark blue
	4	"		"
	Ø	Changes hue	Dark grey	Dark blue
	1	Orange	"	"
1	2	"	"	Changes hue
	3	"	"	Dark blue
	4	"	Changes hue	"
	Ø	Light green	Dark grey	Dark blue
2	1	Changes hue	"	"
	2	Light green	"	Changes hue
	3	"	"	Dark blue
	4	"	Changes hue	"
	Ø	Dark blue	Dark grey	Dark blue
3	1	"	"	"
	2	Change hue	"	Change hue
	3	Dark blue	Dark grey	Dark blue
	4	"	Change hue	"
	Ø			
4	1			
(Same as	2			
COLOR Ø)	3			
	4			

NOTE: A single color listed in the third, fourth, or fifth column indicates the default color for that combination of COLOR and Color Register. For example, in graphics mode 3, a combination of COLOR 1 and Color Register 2 will result in the figure remaining orange, regardless of the value entered for Hue in the SETCOLOR command.

Graphics Mode 4 and 6

Value for COLOR command	Value for Color Register	RESULTS ON SCREEN: Plot points or figure	Background screen	Text window
	Ø	Defaults to color of background	Dark grey	Dark blue
Ø	1	"	"	"
	2	"	"	Changes hue
	3	"	"	Dark blue
	4	"	"	"
	Ø	Changes hue	Dark grey	Dark blue
	1	Orange	"	"
1	2	"	"	Changes hue
	3	"	"	Dark blue
	4	"	"	"
	Ø			
2	1			
(Same as	2			
COLOR Ø)	3			
	4			
	Ø			
3	1			
(Same as	2			
COLOR 1)	3			
	4			
	Ø			
4	1			
(Same as	2			
COLOR Ø)	3			
	4			

NOTE: A single color listed in the third, fourth, or fifth column indicates the default color for that combination of COLOR and Color Register. For example, in graphics mode 3, a combination of COLOR 1 and Color Register 2 will result in the figure remaining orange, regardless of the value entered for Hue in the SETCOLOR command.

APPENDIX E

The GTIA Chip: Advances and the Future

The design of the ATARI 400 and 800 computers provides superior sound and graphics, among personal computers. This is partly because, while other personal computers have tried to include the normal functions of the computer as well as the sound and graphics in one processing unit (often called a chip), ATARI uses separate chips for sound and graphics.

As this book was going to press, ATARI announced the existence of a new chip, the GTIA chip, on all ATARI 400 and ATARI 800 computers released in 1982.

The GTIA will replace the CTIA chip currently controlling graphics displays in the ATARI 400 and 800 computers. The GTIA functions are the same as the CTIA chip in graphics modes 0 through 8. However, three new graphics modes are available with the new chip: graphics modes 9, 10, and 11. These additional modes are graphics modes only; no text can be displayed on the screen. Points plotted on the screen in these modes are rectangular in shape, about four times wider than they are high. Using graphics modes 9 through 11 will allow for a greater variety of hues and luminance on the screen.

Although the graphics capability of the machine will be greatly enhanced, most of these functions are not executed in BASIC. The new chip does not affect functions of the graphics mode, COLOR, or SETCOLOR commands described in this book.

If you are, or may become, a more advanced programmer and would like more information about the GTIA chip, we suggest that you consult the publication *DE RE ATARI* by Chris Crawford, which is available through the ATARI Program Exchange (Part #90008, $19.95 plus $2.50 for shipping and handling). The address is:

Atari Program Exchange
P. O. Box 427
155 Moffett Park Drive
Sunnyvale, CA 94086

Good luck with your ATARI Sound and Graphics program.

INDEX